Land Value Taxation in Britain

Land Value Taxation in Britain
Experience and Opportunities

OWEN CONNELLAN

with contributing authors

Nathaniel Lichfield, Frances Plimmer and Tony Vickers

Lincoln Institute of Land Policy
Cambridge, Massachusetts

Library of Congress Cataloging-in-Publication Data

Connellan, Owen.
   **Land value taxation in Britain : experience and opportunities / by Owen
Connellan with contributing authors Nathaniel Lichfield, Frances Plimmer,
and Tony Vickers.**
      p. cm.
   Includes bibliographical references and index.
   ISBN 1-55844-157-3 (pbk.)
   1. Land value taxation--Great Britain. I. Title.

HJ4337.C66 2004
336.22'5--dc22

                                                              2004001634

Project management: Julia Gaviria, Lincoln Institute of Land Policy
Copyediting: Deborah Kreuze
Design and production: David Gerratt, DG Communications
Cover photo: Whitehall at Dusk, London. Andrew Ward/Life File, Getty Images
Printing: Webcom Ltd., Toronto, Ontario, Canada

Contents

SUPPLEMENTAL MATERIAL

ADDITIONAL MATERIAL

Available on the Lincoln Institute Web site: www.lincolninst.edu

Foreword

Land Value Taxation in Britain provides us with a summary of British experience in land taxation, and of the thinking that has guided attitudes and actions on this point. It offers valuable assistance in making important tax policy choices by giving us information about local government finance and land use. In practice, the decisions about such topics embody a variety of elements, but often tax aspects are central.

Local government financing influences the quantity and quality of public services that are crucial to the way we, and our children, live. Whether or not the term *crisis* can be properly applied to local financing may be argued, but there is no doubt that many British and American citizens live in communities with troubling financial problems. How, then, are desirable and necessary services to be paid for? This volume gives us insights, drawing on the British example.

The choices made about taxes have nonrevenue effects. When taxes increase, the nonrevenue aspects warrant increased attention. Although British policies are in flux, property (real estate) taxation remains an important element of local finance. It influences the physical community as it develops over the years; and, of course, the structures of the community will influence the continuing ability to pay for government.

The British government under Margaret Thatcher, after considerable controversy, made sweeping changes to the traditional system of local government financing. The new policies aroused such opposition that they were largely abolished before being fully implemented. It was a missed opportunity that the discussions surrounding the policies did not focus on land value, on the unique characteristics of land-based tax, or on the possible role of property taxes in community planning. The present volume will help focus these issues in future debate.

Taxes related to real property continue to play a role in financing local government. Business properties are treated differently than residential properties. The system functions, but could be improved. Taxes and systems of government finance can be changed, for better or worse, by the men and women who have created today's institutions. But change in government does not come in the way that "the market" brings change. Taxes will not continually improve themselves through the competition of the marketplace. Taxes are legislated, and past legislation has produced the laws that we have today. How then can the system be improved? What proposed changes would have desirable effects?

One proposal for improving property taxation goes by the designation "land value taxation" (LVT). The concept is defined with some flexibility. LVT recalls Henry George's proposals (without any presumption of being a "single" tax) to capture unearned increments of land prices to help pay for government, which have a long history in both the U.K. and the U.S. And the concerns motivating these proposals are alive in both countries. But the case for LVT is broader than merely capturing such gains for the government, and it is developed well in this volume.

American readers should recall that in Britain a single body, Parliament, makes rules that cover the whole country (with the exception of certain prescribed powers devolved to the Scottish and Welsh legislatures, but currently in suspension in Northern Ireland). Land taxation has been something of a national concern, and for generations there have been debate and effort to inspire action that would apply across the country. (In the U.S., local independence, subject to state government, stands out.) The British Parliament has made three ambitious efforts since World War II to guide land use. This book recounts the results, which fall far short of the hopes. But the story will continue, and there must be action. Town and country planning requires decisions. The positive results might include paying some of the costs with benefits to land. And LVT can be utilized as a means of paying for local government.

Owen Connellan and the contributing authors here summarize the history of LVT. Yet, *Land Value Taxation in Britain* is more than bare history; it can help in making history.

— *C. Lowell Harriss*
Professor Emeritus of Economics, Columbia University

Preface & Acknowledgements

Land Value Taxation in Britain: Experience and Opportunities is designed to enhance research, particularly on taxation matters in the U.K. and other countries, and also for the general reader who does not necessarily have a background in economics or taxation. The book offers a survey of land value taxation as experienced in Britain and serves as a starting point for readers who wish to enquire further into various topics raised in the text.

In order to provide the most complete survey of British land taxation, and given the constraints of a single publication, the Lincoln Institute has utilised both the book format and its Web site to make this information available to the broadest audience possible. All appendices to the book's text as well as some supporting annexes and tables, which are not included in the print edition, may be found on the Lincoln Institute Web site: www.lincolninst.edu. The book's text, with appropriate links, is posted in its entirety on the Web site as well. Several Lincoln Institute working papers that were used as source material are also available for downloading. The reader is encouraged to explore the wealth of material presented both on the Web and in this volume.

Land Value Taxation in Britain has been enhanced by contributions from Nathaniel Lichfield, Frances Plimmer and Tony Vickers. I would also like to acknowledge James Robertson, who made valuable comments on the debate over eco-taxes and taxation shift. My appreciation also goes to those who made observations on drafts of previous working papers as they emerged: Asli Ball, John Corkindale, Roy Douglas, Riël Franzsen, Malcolm Grant, C. Lowell Harriss, Mark Jackson, David Jenkins, Henry Law, William McCluskey, Greg McGill, David Mills, Dick Netzer, Sarah Sayce and David Westfall. And my special thanks go to Joan Youngman, Jane Malme, Ann LeRoyer and Julia Gaviria, of the Lincoln Institute, for their encouragement and help in getting this book into publication. Finally, I thank those who have generously given permission to cite references, extensive quotations and extracts in the book itself, particularly Mrs. Pauline C. Prest, widow of Professor A.R. Prest, author of *The Taxation of Urban Land* (1981), and also the Institute of Fiscal Studies.

— *Owen Connellan*

■ PART ONE ■
Introduction

■ CHAPTER ONE

What This Book Is All About

This book is about taxation—in particular, land value taxation (LVT)—
and its possible repercussions beyond its role in generating government
revenue. Our examination encompasses both the practical operation of
LVT and its moral background and ethical rationale. We crystallize our
exploration around a case study of Britain,[1] which has a long historical association
with LVT, and where past attempts to introduce various forms of LVT have
resulted in mixed degrees of success and failure. From this analysis we anticipate
future prospects for such uses of LVT in Britain and elsewhere.

We do all of this against the current background of "taxation shift": a sea
change away from production taxes and on to various exactions that could be
made for the use and abuse of natural resources, including land. Here we are
entering the realms of eco-taxation and issues affecting the sustainability of the
planet, and we consider whether LVT has a rightful place among these important measures currently under debate. The significance of these issues speaks for
itself, and LVT is argued, by its supporters at least, as an ideal vehicle to encourage new approaches to taxation at perhaps a historical turning point. Finally, and
for the future, this book seeks to open up a challenge for discussion from what
is basically designed as an educational text and a reference source.

But why study land value taxation in Britain? This question is particularly
pertinent when we admit that Britain has not, at any time over the last century
or so, evolved a system of LVT that has found plausible general acceptance and
has worked to reasonable expectations. The answer is that if we examine the history of the many legislative and administrative attempts to introduce and use
LVT for the benefit of the community (see Chapter 5 *et seq*) and analyse "what
went right and what went wrong," we can arrive at an arguable baseline from

---

1. The term *Britain* refers in general terms to Great Britain (England, Wales and Scotland). There clearly
   are variations in operation between the countries.

which to put forward LVT proposals for Britain that might go right and perhaps not go wrong. Britain's long history of property taxation and wealth of property valuation expertise strengthen the case for this particular study, not only for its importance to Britain, but also for possible implications regarding LVT in other parts of the world (Connellan 1997, 1999, 2000a; Connellan et al. 2003).

The main objectives of this book (using Britain as a case study) are to explain the nature and background of land value taxation; to consider the ways in which LVT may be particularly relevant at the present time; and to evaluate its future.

The Notion of Land Value Taxation

What is land value taxation? How is it applied? Is it a fairer method of taxation? And what is its current importance?

LVT has both a particular and generalised meaning. In particular, LVT refers to levying annual taxes on specific parcels of land in order to gather revenue for local government (this is referred to as *site value rating* [SVR] in Britain). In essence, this is an attempt to redistribute the rates burden (i.e., the extant British property tax) and collect local government revenues on a more equitable basis (Clarke 1965, 78). The generalised meaning of LVT includes not only the afore-mentioned particular meaning but also policies and measures aimed at recouping to the community (called *value capture* or *betterment*) some proportion of the increases in land value that can be attributed to community activity that generates development. In addition, it takes in cognate methods for recovering infrastructure costs, whereby authorities are empowered to levy from landowners and developers some element of the cost of infrastructure (both physical and social) arising out of particular development projects.

One often-used category of land value capture for the community not included above, which we have termed *recoupment via purchase*, may be seen as a form of land banking by public authorities. This is not, strictly speaking, the same as levying taxes without ownership itself, but it has been well described as "pre-empting the accrual of value" (Grant 1999, 67).

Among the other disparate forms of taxation and recoupment of land values (which we shall examine in more detail in Chapters 5–8)—that is, targeting cap-ital (development) gains, recouping infrastructure costs, and even recouping land values through forward purchasing of sites by the government—there is evident confusion. As has been pointed out by Blundell (1993, 22), an annual tax (such as SVR) should pick up all increases in land value over time as opposed to the one-off hits by value capture exactions consequent upon certain trigger events.

However, let us, for the moment, stay with the simplest and most straight-forward form of LVT—an annual tax for funding some government expen-ditures. How does this annual tax operate? It is applied by means of a value attributed to the land in question—by an assessment either of annual rent or of capital value, from which tax base an annual tax is levied on a percentage (or millage) basis.

But how does LVT differ from other forms of property taxes? First, the tax is on the land itself; this differs from the main form of extant property tax around the world, which is based on assessing the combined value of land, buildings and improvements thereon rather than on the land per se. Second, the onus of the tax is generally on the owner and not the occupier (as may be the case in some countries).

Is LVT fairer and more equitable than other forms of property taxes? LVT's proponents have certainly affirmed this through the ages, including Henry George (1839–1897), an American economist and social philosopher and a leading spokesman for the cause. A detailed review of this issue follows in the next chapter, which deals with economic theory and principles.

Why Is LVT Now Relevant and Important?

It can be argued that it is now timely and appropriate to contemplate an introduction of LVT, especially into Britain. In support, various current pressures can be identified as accumulating for a change in taxation, particularly towards a more equitable distribution of the rates burden (property tax) and thus a fairer collection of local government revenues. These mooted changes also include widening the tax base to bring in properties presently unrated and not caught up in the current British property tax, e.g., empty, derelict and unused properties. Such pressures arise from the present incidence of devolving governing and taxation powers to Scotland, Wales and (when eventually restored to) Northern Ireland, and also to the activities of various influential special-interest and political groups (e.g., "Greens," Scottish nationalists, liberal democrats and even active "Georgist" organisations).

As has been pointed out by James Robertson (1998a, 1998b, 1999) and others, there is a growing movement towards taxation shift, that is to say, to reduce taxes on enterprise, production and income sources and move taxation towards the "cost of using the environment." This, in turn, is connected to the whole theme of sustainability of the environment and sustainable development.[2] But it is also relevant at this point to note that Robertson has already recommended a whole raft of radical policies to include eco-tax reform and site value land taxation, among the connected parts of a larger package based on:

- introducing a range of taxes and charges on the use of common resources and values, including but not limited to energy and the site value of land;

---

2. Sustainable development is defined as "meeting the needs of the present without compromising the ability of future generations to meet their own needs" (WCED 1987).

- reducing, and perhaps eventually abolishing, taxes and charges on employment, incomes, profits, value added and capital;
- reducing taxes on incomes and profits earned from useful work and enterprise, the value they add, and what they contribute to the common good; and
- increasing taxes and charges that reflect the value they subtract by their use of common resources, including land, energy and the capacity of the environment to absorb pollution and waste.

As indicated above, the so-called eco-taxes[3] are increasingly a part of this taxation shift, and the question of their compatibility with LVT has previously been examined by Lichfield and Connellan (2000c). They concluded that these two forms of taxes, although different in history and application, should be able to coexist in mutual harmony and interdependence.

But such extensions of the application and range of LVT are also heralded in the next chapter, when referring to contemporary views on Georgism, particularly the assertion from Solow:

> The best way to keep George's ideas alive and effective is to develop and refine them, and to extend their range of relevance to issues of land use, urban form, and taxation, including many aspects that could never have crossed George's mind. The range of possible activities is very broad. . . . The list could be very long; this random selection is intended to indicate only how diverse it could be. (1997, 14)

His statement reminds us that we are dealing with a still-developing theme of ideas that requires continuous reexamination for its relevance to modern circumstances, the principle of which governs the structure of this book, as described below.

Structure of the Book

To deal with the above-described matters sequentially, the book is structured in three parts.

Part I presents Britain as the case study country and introduces the theory and principles of land value taxation.

Part II reviews "The British Experience." Chapters 3 and 4 describe general taxation, including current taxes on land and property for local government revenues. Chapter 5 reviews more than 100 years of attempts to introduce LVT in Britain—from 1890 to the present day. Chapters 6 through 8 describe three

---

3. Eco-taxation here follows the definition used by the European Commission (ATW Research 1996), namely, that it is based on a physical unit (or proxy thereof) of something that has proven specific negative impact on the environment. It can be a tax (unrequited payments to government) or a charge (requited payments for which a service is provided by some public body generally in proportion to payment made), and these are examples of economic and financial instruments that are designed to modify market behaviour with a view to achieving government objectives (DETR 1994).

methods of capital value capture for the benefit of the community that are supplementary to annual land value taxation as such, namely recoupment via ownership, betterment via the town and country planning system, and contributions to infrastructure costs.

Part III, "Opportunities for Future Land Value Taxation," introduces prospective proposals for Britain, starting with the annual form of LVT (site value rating) in Chapters 9 and 10. Chapters 11, 12 and 13 review proposals for the three supplementary methods of LVT. Chapter 14 discusses how compatibility can be achieved between LVT and planning, particularly in the case of Britain, where special kinds of development control are practiced. Chapter 15 explores political prospects and feasibility of LVT in Britain. "Final Review" (Chapter 16) looks at all that has gone before and what might lie ahead, including LVT's relationship to taxation shift and eco-taxes, as well as the key questions emerging: What does all this mean? And how important is it?

Appendices A, B, C, D, E and F are fuller versions of the body text in certain chapters, for closer study and more detailed reference. These documents may be found on the Lincoln Institute Web site: www.lincolninst.edu.

CHAPTER TWO

Theory and Principles of Land Value Taxation

T his chapter summarises the economic and moral thinking that argues the case for land value taxation, dealing first with economic theory and then with the moral aspects and principles that emerge from that discussion, with a focus on the influence of Henry George.

Principles of General Taxation

Before pursuing the economic background of LVT, however, let us first take a brief look at some of the established principles of general taxation. Here we are reminded that, in examining any tax-raising proposal, it is almost traditional to revisit the precepts of one of the early founders of those principles.

Adam Smith (1776) first systematised the rules that should govern a rational system of taxation, and Stanlake summarised these rules as follows:

> Taxes should be based on the individual's ability to pay in that there must be equality of sacrifice—as instanced by progressive taxes, certainty with knowledge of how much tax, when and how it must be paid and not be subject to arbitrary demands, convenience in collection as to form and timing, and economy in that costs of collection should be small in relation to the total revenue. (1989, 433)

Smith describes these maxims as having "evident justice and utility." So they may have, but the fact was insufficiently appreciated in Smith's time (Raphael 1985, 83). However, the ability to pay was viewed by Smith as conditional on income *actually being received* ("revenue which they respectively enjoy"), rather than potential income that could be imputed to the possession of a revenue-yielding resource (Harrison 1983, 28). This point has later important implications in deriving a workable methodology for land value taxation, as we shall see in Chapters 9 and 10.

Before moving on from the initial precepts of Smith, it is pertinent to this review that modern criteria of tax systems also include revenue productivity and considerations of social justice. As submitted in the *Encyclopaedia Britannica*, a tax system should provide adequate revenues to cover government expenditures and should be capable of producing more on short notice when circumstances require (1997, vol. 11, 584). Conceptions of social justice may require, in addition, that taxes be more or less progressively redistributive of income, wealth or both. Furthermore, as governments have come to play a larger part in controlling their national economies, taxes have been used to moderate cyclical economic fluctuations, to promote a higher level of economic activity, and to affect the application of economic resources. All these factors have implications in our subsequent examination of LVT.

Economic Theory: Why Tax Land?

The main form of extant property tax around the world is based on a combination of land, buildings and improvements thereon, so let us now focus on land itself as a particular source of taxation and on the fundamental question: Why tax land?

The answer to this question has been heavily explored in economic theory over the last two centuries. As Prest (1981, 8) indicates, such a tax was favoured by the Physiocrats, a group of economic thinkers, in eighteenth-century France on the grounds that only in agriculture does a country have a surplus *and* source of wealth, so that there is a case for levying an *impôt unique*[1] on land rents. As we shall examine later, the Physiocrats in essence set out to exhibit the way that products of agriculture (then considered the primary source of wealth) would, in a state of perfect liberty, be distributed among different classes of the community (Robinson 1991, 6).

Following this stimulus, the topic was explored, for both rural and urban land, by an array of other classical economists including Smith, David Ricardo, John Stuart Mill, Alfred Marshall, Arthur Pigou and Henry George. On the whole, theories are consistently in favour of taxing land, but there are important variations. The total view can be briefly summarised here by referring to the historical analysis of the Simes Committee of Enquiry (1952, 6) in its report *The Rating of Site Values* for the British government. (The committee's findings are discussed in Chapter 5.)

It is worth emphasising that the Simes Committee was considering the taxation of site (land) values, ignoring the value of any improvements such as buildings, fences or crops: the land valued as a bare site available for development in accordance with its situation and other physical characteristics but subject to the extant system of planning control (Clarke 1965). The committee concluded

---

1. Or *impôt inique*, as described by Voltaire.

that the case for taxation of economic rent[2] arising from site (land) values rests upon the following propositions:

- that it is unearned income, brought into existence not by anything that the owner, as such, has done but by the activities of the community generally;
- that a tax on it does not curtail the supply of goods and services and raise their price as many other taxes do; and
- that, in particular, it is a means of relieving the burden imposed by rates (extant property taxes in Britain) as presently levied upon dwelling houses, shops and other buildings and improvements to land.

From these propositions the Simes Committee concluded that there might therefore be a prima facie case for a tax on such economic rent as a source of local revenue. As already indicated, such a case for accruing increased values in land to the community rather than to landowners relies partly on the argument that it is public expenditure on supporting infrastructure that is a primary cause of such increases. Consequently, those public efforts should be recognised in a form of taxation redress to the community.

LVT and Economic Rent

The fact that the total supply of land in a country is fixed, and the view that the income derived from the ownership of raw land is a kind of "unearned" surplus, continues to lend support for measures to tax economic rent. As Stanlake points out, in many countries, expanding populations and rising incomes have increased the demand for land, and landowners have benefited from rising land prices, although they may have contributed little or nothing to the increase in the value of their land. Furthermore, "the main attraction of a tax on economic rent is the arguable case that the whole of the tax would fall on the landlords" (Stanlake 1989, 284).

Kay and King also indicate that one of the oldest ideas in public finance is that there are advantages in basing tax on economic rent. Most people are familiar with what is meant by the rent of land or buildings, but the concept of rent in economics has a specific technical meaning: it is the amount that a factor of production earns over and above what it could earn in its next best use. They conclude that "therefore rent is the result of the scarcity of particular factors of production and therefore rent could be taxed, or otherwise reduced, without any economic distortion arising" (Kay and King 1990, 177).

---

2. Pareto defined economic rent as "a payment over and above what is necessary to keep it in its present employment" (Whitehead 1992, 200), but see also the later sections in this chapter.

Starting from the basic premise that the best price (i.e., rent) one could get for land would be determined by demand and supply, Whitehead then develops the argument, previously cited, by examining the effect of taxation on economic rents when a factor is in inelastic supply, as in the instance of land. He maintains that the landlord owners are able to command economic rents and that imposing the tax will not cause any change in demand or supply. The tax will have to be borne entirely by the supplier (the landlords) and will reduce the benefits being enjoyed hitherto, and consequently, "landowners earning economic rents cannot alter their position, which is already the most profitable one, and the tax will simply cream off their profits" (Whitehead 1992, 413).

Whitehead's argument supports the view that a tax on land values cannot increase the market price[3]—the tax must fall on the landowners and must, therefore, reduce the revenue they receive as landlords—but he also points out that "economic rent is not unique to land; it accrues to any factor, which is fixed in supply and faces an increasing demand" (Whitehead 1992, 414). The differentiation appears to hinge on whether these other factors can generally be increased in supply over time as contrasted with the comparatively finite nature of land supply. If supply can, over time, respond to increasing demand, then this must reduce the economic rent element. But, as we have already seen, this is difficult to achieve with the supply of land.

Arguments for LVT

The various arguments put forward to support land value taxation are succinctly enumerated in the *Encyclopaedia Britannica* (1997, vol. 28, 416), particularly the argument that much of what is paid for the use of land reflects socially created demand and is not a payment to bring land into existence. The community can capture in land taxes some of the values it has created, including those resulting from streets, schools and other facilities. This, it is maintained, would be a more equitable way of financing local government. Another argument is that the revenue from a tax on land would permit reducing taxes on buildings, which tend to deter new construction. A third argument is that higher land taxes would make for a more efficient use of land.

These arguments are developed on the supposition that a heavier tax would also change the conditions of ownership. The total collected from users would not change, but private owners of land would retain less and the public treasury more. The price system would still affect land use, subject to planning control. Taxes on improvements could then be reduced greatly. The tax relief on dilapidated buildings would be slight, but for high-quality buildings the reduction could be large relative to net return on investment. More buildings, new and

---

3. Although the market price may well decrease over time by a process of capitalisation of the tax.

better ones, would be supplied. Modernisation and maintenance of existing buildings would become more profitable. Thus, in the long run, it is argued, landowners would receive less of the increments in land values and the public would receive more. Socially created values would then be channelled into governmental rather than private uses. Taxes could be related more closely to the cost of governmental services.

However, as Prest (1981, 11) indicates, there are contrary views. Opponents of LVT point out that the unearned increment in land value has been capitalised in the purchase price, and they question the fairness of imposing a heavy tax on present land values for which owners have paid in good faith. They doubt the ability of assessors to make fair enough appraisals to support much heavier taxes on land. They also doubt that land alone, excluding buildings, would be an adequate tax base. Feldstein (1977) argues that not the whole of the land tax burden falls on landowners nor do relative outputs remain unchanged, thus expressing some doubt on the traditional neutrality of land taxation with respect to resource allocation. In turn, there are counterarguments to these views, as will emerge in later chapters.

Combining Economic and Moral Rationales

As noted earlier, there exists a relationship between classical economic thought and the moral aspects of land taxation. We now look more closely at these influences.

The ethical arguments concerning the ownership and rights over land were pronounced in the eighteenth century onwards, when the French Physiocrats began to articulate the economic and moral rationales for land taxation. Land had been a recognisable target for tax gatherers since ancient times, but more modern taxation rationales were developed from the thinking of the Physiocrats and refined by such exponents as Smith, Ricardo, Mill, Marshall and Pigou. Henry George, with his plea for a single tax on land as a panacea for all economic and fiscal problems, made the biggest impact in the nineteenth century, and despite peer criticism and academic strictures, his influence remains today. We now turn again to these influential thinkers in more detail.

The Physiocrats were founded by François Quesnay (1694–1774), court physician to Madame Pompadour and Louis XV, but his followers preferred to be known as *economistes*. However, as further explained in the *Encyclopaedia Britannica* (1997, vol. 9, 414), the term *physiocrats* became current only in the nineteenth century, and this school of *economistes* was characterised chiefly by a belief that government policy should not interfere with the operation of natural economic laws. Generally regarded as the first scientific school of economics, it considered land as being the source of all wealth. Physiocrats, emphasising the role of nature, envisaged a society in which natural economic and moral laws would have full play and in which positive law would be in harmony with natural law. They pictured a predominantly agricultural society and therefore attacked mercantilism. Given their assumptions and the social system they desired, the Physiocrats were logical and systematic. They rationalised medieval economic ideals, employing to that end the more modern philosophical and scientific methods. As to practical outcomes, a land tax was established by the French Revolutionary Constituent Assembly in December 1790, which also followed Physiocratic concepts, but it eventually foundered.

Adam Smith (1723–1790) distinguished the varying types of taxes on land and traced out their differing effects. He also set in motion the train of reasoning about the taxation of urban land rents, saying, "ground-rents, and the ordinary rent of land, are therefore, perhaps, the species of revenue which can best bear to have a peculiar tax imposed upon them" (Smith 1776, 843–844).

Prest summarises Smith's arguments as follows:

- Taxes on urban land rents are neutral in their resource allocation effects.
- It is fair to tax away surpluses that are more due to extraneous circumstances than to individual efforts.
- People should pay for government actions and services, which are to their advantage. (Prest 1981, 9)

However, Smith would not accept the solution that a tax levied on the market value of *all* land would constitute a continuous pressure on the possessors and would induce those who possessed land to play the game of competition and cooperation. It is true that Smith regarded land as "peculiarly" suitable for taxation, since such a tax falls on an economic surplus and could not be passed on to consumers in the price of goods. But he resisted the application of the tax on the value of *all* land. In fact, he explicitly opposed a tax on the rental income that could be imputed to idle land (Harrison 1983, 28–29).

David Ricardo (1772–1823) is generally attributed with formulating the law of rent. He argued that the rent of land is determined by the excess of its produce over that which in the same application can be secured from the least productive land in use. Ricardo also supported a tax on rent and bolstered the idea of a single tax on land (Robinson 1991, 7).

But Prest (1981, 910) makes the point that, although no one can fail to recognise the immensity of Ricardo's intellectual achievement in isolating the concept of economic rent and attaching it to "the original and indestructible powers of the soil" (Ricardo 1951, 67), his contribution to the subject of urban land taxation is relatively limited. In his comments on Smith, Ricardo was content to say, "The effect of these taxes [on ground-rents and the ordinary rent of land] would be much as Adam Smith has described" (Ricardo 1951, 204). Furthermore, having developed the concept of intensive and extensive margins of cultivation with rural land, Ricardo did not apply them in the context of urban land.

It used to be common practice, following Ricardo, to define land as "the original and inexhaustible powers of the soil," but, as noted by Lipsey (1989, 286), Ricardo wrote before it was widely known that many present-day deserts had once been fertile areas. Lipsey also writes that, in his famous argument, Ricardo maintained that the rent of corn land was high because the price of corn was high and not vice versa (1989, 300–301). Lipsey points out that modern students of economics will recognise in the Ricardian argument the idea of *derived demand*. Given the fixed supply of land, its price depended on the demand for land, which was itself a function of the price of corn. Rent, which originally referred to the payment for the use of land, thus became the term for a surplus payment to a factor over and above what was necessary to keep it in its present use. The concept of economic rent, the surplus of total earnings over transfer earnings, is analogous to the modern economists' concept of profit as a surplus over opportunity cost.

In a further explanation of the concept of economic rent, Stanlake (1989, 280) emphasises that the essence of Ricardo's theory is that the supply of land, unlike the supply of capital and labour, cannot change in response to a change in demand. Land has no supply price. The amount available does not depend on the market price; higher prices do not lead to larger quantities being supplied, and falling prices do not reduce the actual supply. The *supply price* of a factor may be defined as the minimum reward necessary to retain a factor in its current employment. Any payment to a factor of production that is greater than its supply price is a kind of surplus, and it is this surplus that is known as economic rent.

But Stanlake also reiterates the argument that most land can be put to different uses and that the "supply of land for any one use is not fixed" (1989, 280). Removing the assumptions does not invalidate the idea of economic rent as a surplus, but modern economists maintain that this concept can be applied to other factors of production besides land. Whenever a factor is earning more than its supply price, it is receiving a part of its income in the form of economic rent; this happens when demand increases and the supply cannot fully and readily respond to the increased demand. But this does not recognise the unique feature of land: with minor exceptions (e.g., tall buildings or coastal reclamations), the increased demand cannot create an increased supply.

In summary then, and in consideration of the concept of attributing value to land, for a factor of production to have a cash value it must have utility, be capable of ownership and be limited in supply. Turner (1977, 1) again illustrates these principles with respect to land by looking at Ricardo's theory of rent, but with a specific proviso. The economist usually uses the word *rent* to refer to *economic* rent, the surplus earned by a factor of production over the minimum necessary to bring it into production. But using the legal definition of land as real property and including buildings and other improvements that the economist would regard as capital rather than land, the income received from the land in the form of *contract* rent will include elements of interest, or return on capital.

John Stuart Mill (1806–1873) declared that rents were "created by circumstances" and justifiably could have been expropriated from the time of Adam and Eve onwards. However, Mill saw two obstacles to taxing rents at an extreme rate. First, it is not always easy to distinguish between the elements of current values, due to private endeavour and "circumstances." Second, the present owners of land may be not the people who have drawn rents over the centuries but recent purchasers, who bought at market values based on expectations of future rent levels free from confiscatory taxation. A third obstacle is that there are many other cases where people may enjoy monopoly-type surpluses, and, as Prest concludes, "it is hard to see the equity case for taxing one lot of monopoly rents specially without taxing as many of the others as one can" (1981, 28).

Mill's solution was to ascertain the present value of all land, urban and rural; thereafter, all future increments in value could be safely taxed at a high rate, unless it could be shown that they were specifically due to the endeavour of individuals. In other words, the principle was to tax unexpected windfalls in land values. In the end, a land tax could be thought of as a public rent-charge or a substitute for the state's retaining part of the land (Prest 1981, 12).

Alfred Marshall (1842–1924) also contributed to the theory of urban rents by demonstrating that Ricardo's notion of intensive and extensive margins of cultivation to agricultural land could also be applied as a principle to urban land. Urban site values, like agricultural land values, were determined by demand levels, and for Marshall, as for Ricardo, land was distinct from all other agents of production because of its long-term fixity of supply and because the whole of the return on it was a surplus. Marshall argued that taxing site value was analogous to taxing monopoly profits in that there was surplus, which could be tapped without any deleterious effects on resource allocation. Taxes on site values would reduce these excess profits of owners, but that would be all.

From this analysis, Prest (1981, 16) concludes that Marshall distinguished three different solutions. First, the state should buy land plus buildings at full market price. Second, the state should purchase the inherent value of the soil. Third, all land should become state property 100 years hence—a plan Marshall deemed to be less objectionable than the others.

Arthur Pigou (1877–1959) in 1909 made a clear distinction between taxes on the public value of land (i.e., LVT as an annual tax) and taxes on windfalls (i.e., unexpected increments in land values), and he declared himself in favour of both taxes, arguing from both economic theory and practical experience in other countries. In the case of site value taxes, the main theoretical plank was their neutrality from a resource-allocation standpoint, essentially along the lines of Ricardian rent theory. The case for taxes on windfall increments was held to be similar to that for wartime excess profits taxation: if increments arose that were neither foreseen nor due to the recipient's effort, they were ideal objects of taxation from a resource allocation viewpoint, and they were also likely to be distributionally commendable.

Prest sums this up rather neatly in his assessment of Pigou's distinctive approach: "[It seems] fair to summarize Pigou's position as being a synthesis of Marshall and J. S. Mill in that he could claim the authority of the former (but not the latter) for arguing for taxation of site values but the authority of the latter (though not the former) for taxing increments in land value" (1981, 18–19).

Distinctive Theory of Henry George: The Single Tax

In *Progress and Poverty* (1879), Henry George, an American who was probably the best-known exponent of land value taxation, drew upon economic analysis in the tradition of Ricardo and Mill to argue persuasively for a single tax on land and the abolition of other taxes, which then were predominantly levied on other property (Harrison 1983, chs. 15–16). George argued that since land values were exclusively due to general forces, whether of a natural or social character, landlords had no moral right to land values, and so there was no case for their being allowed to retain existing rents or the increments that were likely to eventuate in the future as economies expanded (Prest 1981, 13).

George originally advocated replacing all existing taxes with a single tax upon land values. Supporters of George argued that since land is a fixed resource, the economic rent is a product of the growth of the economy and not of individual effort, and society would be justified in recovering it to support the costs of government. (They accepted Ricardo's view that a tax on economic rent could not be shifted forward; as we have already noted, the main attraction of such a tax is that the whole of the tax would fall on the landowners.) George's supporters also argued that a single tax on land would eliminate taxes on buildings, which would stimulate construction and economic growth, and that a single tax would be very simple to administer.

Impact of Henry George in Britain

During the 1880s, George visited Britain five times; three of those visits were extended speaking tours. Among progressive thinkers his impact was considerable. Testimonials by Bernard Shaw, Sidney and Beatrice Webb, H.G. Wells and other eminent Fabians explicitly credit George as the most potent single instrument in converting both individuals and the working class itself to trade unionism and socialism (Lawrence et al. 1992, 57; Prest 1981, 14). (Lawrence points out the interesting paradox that Henry George, the apostle of frontier individualism and free trade, should have gone down in history as the godfather of British socialism [Lawrence et al. 1992, 83].)

By the late 1880s, the radicals of Britain's Liberal Party allied themselves with George in supporting land taxation, an alliance that affected legislation some 20 years later in the Finance Act of 1909–1910 and then much later on, from the Labour Party, in the Finance Act of 1931. (Although enacted, these measures were abandoned before they could be fully implemented.)

Despite his wide influence, George did have to contend with much adverse comment from current and later economic critics. Marshall dubbed him "a poet, not a scientific thinker" (Stigler 1969); Marx said, "theoretically the man is thoroughly backward" (Barker 1955, 356); and J. M. Keynes attributed George's thinking to "the underworld of economics" (Prest 1981, 21). But Schumpeter, the doyen of the history of economic thought, frames George more generously. In recalling "[a] few of those men who helped to prepare the ground for developments from the 1880s on," Schumpeter states:

> [W]e cannot afford to pass by the economist whose individual success with the public was greater than that of all the others on our list, Henry George. The points about him that are relevant for a history of analysis are these. He was a self-taught economist, but he *was* an economist. In the course of his life, he acquired most of the knowledge and the ability to handle an economic argument that he could have acquired by academic training as it then was. In this he differed to his advantage from most men who proffered panaceas. Barring his panacea [the Single Tax] and the phraseology connected with it, he was a very orthodox economist and extremely conservative as to methods. They were those of the English " classics," A. Smith being his particular favourite. Marshall and Böhm-Bawerk he failed to understand. But up to and including Mill's treatise, he was thoroughly at home in scientific economics; and he shared none of the current misunderstanding or prejudices concerning it. Even the panacea—nationalisation not of land but of the rent of land by a confiscatory tax—benefited by his competence as an economist, for he was careful to frame his "remedy" in such a manner as to cause the minimum injury to the efficiency of the private-enterprise economy. Professional economists who focused attention on the single-tax proposal and condemned Henry George's teaching, root and branch, were hardly just to him. (1954, 864–865)

Contemporary Views on Georgism

More than a century later, the supporters of the Henry George tradition, in various groupings of societies and foundations around the world, are still actively pursuing George's precepts on land taxation and arguing his case. As Lee (1996, 78) points out, the hope for supporters of LVT must lie in promoting their ideals to the general public and educating future politicians to appreciate the merits of such a tax. Several bodies are actively trying to do this in Britain: the Henry George Foundation UK (founded in 1907 as the United Committee for the Taxation of Land Values), the Land Value Taxation Campaign, the Land Policy Council and the Scottish Ogilvie Council.

But the survival is deeper than just the campaign. Lawrence et al. (1992, 56) comment that *Progress and Poverty* had a dramatic impact on George's British economist contemporaries, and although George's theory did not shape economic theory, his ideas were present in the minds of those who did. Fundamentally, his ideas on land taxation persisted even into the minds of twentieth-century economists.

Quite apart from the ongoing campaign for LVT, there is also a contemporary exploration of the relevance of the ideas and philosophy of Henry George to today's issues and problems in the modern world. This is brought out, for example, in the collection of essays, titled *Land Use and Taxation: Applying the Insights of Henry George,* edited by H. James Brown (1997). In his introduction, the editor states:

> Although George could never have anticipated all the changes in real estate development, public finance and property rights that would occur over the following century, the fundamental policy issues that he analyzed are as pressing today as they were 120 years ago. In essence, we are still asking the same question: How do you strike an equitable balance between private property rights and public interest in land?… The essays collected here explain why Henry George's basic ideas about land use and taxation issues still have currency, despite how radically different the world has become as we arrive at the end of the twentieth century…. While they offer markedly different perspectives, each of the authors who contributed to this volume would agree that Henry George's ideas have much to add to the ongoing debate over land policy and taxation issues. (Brown 1997, 1–5)

The questions and answers raised in Brown were echoed in another exploration by the Lincoln Institute at a conference in Arizona, "Land Value Taxation in Contemporary Societies: Can It and Will It Work?" The conclusion states:

> Thus, more research on the use of the most immobile of tax bases is warranted, especially research on the land value tax in the "real world". . . the land value tax should be taken seriously by researchers, not neglected as it has been over the years, as no more than another quaint idea from bygone years. (Netzer 1998, xviii)

Having reviewed the economic and equitable arguments underpinning LVT, including the influence of Henry George, we may proceed to examine the extant tax system in Britain as a background for any proposed introduction of LVT into that system.

PART TWO

The British Experience

CHAPTER THREE

General Taxation and Taxes on Land

We now study the case of Britain in order to consider how LVT (or site value rating [SVR], as it is termed locally) might harmonise with the extant taxation system in the U.K., particularly with respect to the U.K.'s membership in the European Union.

Revenue Currently Raised by U.K. Taxes

How does the U.K. government currently raise revenue?[1] Table 1 shows the sources of government revenue forecasts for 2001–2002, classified into the groups in the HM Treasury financial statement and budget report for 2001, e.g., income tax, national insurance, nondomestic property tax, etc.[2]

Adam and Frayne summarise this Treasury source as follows:

> Total government receipts are forecast to be £398.4 billion in 2001–02, or 40.2% of U.K. GDP. This is equivalent to roughly £8,500 for every adult in the U.K., or £6,600 per person. In 2001–02, the largest single source of revenue for the Government will be taxes on income, both personal and corporate. Approximately £104.1 billion, or 26.1% of total current receipts, will be raised from income tax, with a further £62.6 billion from National Insurance contributions and £37.8 billion from corporation tax. These three sources alone will account for just over 50% of total government revenue. Some £125.0 billion, or 31% of revenue, will be raised by taxes on expenditure, with VAT accounting for £61.3 billion and council tax £14.7 billion. The remainder will be raised by other indirect taxes, including excise duties on petrol, alcohol and tobacco, which will raise a total of around £36.8 billion. Taxes on capital will provide a further £13.0 billion for the exchequer. (2001, 1–2)[3]

---

1. This chapter describes the nature and extent of the general taxation system in the U.K. at present, that is to say, covering England, Wales, Scotland, Northern Ireland and the Scilly Isles, but excluding the Channel Islands and the Isle of Man.

2. A further summary description of the U.K. taxes listed in Table 1 can be found in Annexe 1 to this chapter.

3. A more detailed treatment of this range of U.K. taxes may be found in the IFS (Institute of Fiscal Studies) Briefing Note no. 9, "A Survey of the U.K. Tax System," at www.ifs.org.UK/taxsystem/taxsurvey.pdf.

TABLE 1 Original Analysis of Sources of Government Revenue, 2001–2002 Forecasts

Source of revenue	Forecast 2001–2002 (£bn)	Percentage of total (%)
Income tax (net of income tax credits)[a]	104.1	26.1
National insurance contributions	62.6	15.7
Capital taxes		
Capital gains tax	2.5	0.6
Inheritance tax	2.3	0.6
Stamp duties	8.0	2.0
Value added tax	61.3	15.4
Other indirect taxes		
Petrol duties	22.5	5.6
Tobacco duties	7.6	1.9
Alcohol duties	6.7	1.7
Betting and gaming duties	1.5	0.4
Vehicle excise duty	4.5	1.1
Air passenger duty	1.0	0.3
Insurance premium tax	1.8	0.5
Landfill tax	0.5	0.1
Climate change levy	0.8	0.2
Customs duties and levies	2.1	0.5
Corporation taxes		
Corporation tax	37.8	9.5
Petroleum revenue tax	1.6	0.4
National nondomestic rates	17.5	4.4
Oil royalties	0.6	0.2
Council Tax	14.7	3.7
Other taxes and royalties	9.5	2.4
Interest and dividends	4.8	1.2
Gross operating surplus and rent	20.5	5.1
Other receipts and accounting adjustments	1.4	0.4
Current receipts	**398.4**	**100.0**

[a] Gross income tax minus income tax credits

Source: HM Treasury, *Financial Statement and Budget Report, 2001* (www.hm-treasury.gov.U.K./Budget/Budget_2001/Budget_report).

What Is Land?

Having looked at taxation in the U.K. in general, we now turn specifically to the nature and characteristics of land, and introduce its suitability as a tax vehicle.

Land as Terra Firma

In dealing with landed property taxation, we employ the meaning of *land* as land for development—that element of natural resources that is used, or that could be used, for physical development, that is, change of use via mineral extraction or construction. In that context, *land* is thereby limited to the earth's surface (terra firma), the minerals below the surface, and the air and sun above. It is this meaning of land—that of space—that is the platform for associated socio-economic activities, to produce development and thereby the *development value* that can be taxed.

Land as terra firma is uniquely and significantly different from other economic resources (Lichfield and Darin-Drabkin 1980, 12–13; Gaffney 1994, 39–42). And because it is unique, it attracts policies that are also unique. Land is the platform of all human activities, aside from certain telling exceptions, such as space travel. And because raw land is "God-given" or a "gift of Nature," its original qualities are available without any human activity whatsoever. However, human activity is usually needed for improvements that facilitate human use of land: infrastructure and buildings. Land also has unique qualities as a factor of production: it is fixed in location, it is immobile and immovable, and the supply of it cannot be expanded (with only minor exceptions such as reclamation). In addition, land has a special place in society, in that, for example, no state can be said to be independent that does not control its own land, and no individual can be said to be independent who does not have freedom of access to a part of that land. It is over possession of land that people have fought wars for centuries.

Because land holds this special significance, societies throughout history have found it necessary to restrict absolute ownership of any portion of the land against the rest of society; they have not done this for automobiles, television sets and so on. Thus, it has been generally accepted that any individual's use of terra firma need be subservient to some overriding control, for example, by tribal chiefs, nation-states, federal governments or international agreements. Of course, this notion of land's special place in society also raises the question of its special relationship with taxation, but before we explore this, let us look at land in a different capacity.

Land as a Legal Concept and as Construed for LVT

In physical terms, land combines the raw earth and mankind's improvements to it. In British legal parlance, "land includes buildings and other structures, land covered by water, and any estate, interest, easement, servitude or right in or over land" (Interpretation Act 1978, s. 5 and Schedule 1). So, in our interpretation of extant land taxation, it is relevant to consider how far the ownership and/or occupation of land, as this form of property is usually understood in the context of LVT, is already subject to taxation of one sort or another. (We examine this aspect of interdependence later in this chapter.) However, there are also other definitions of land more concerned with providing a vehicle for LVT, and for our purposes here we adopt the following definition from Lichfield and Connellan:

The share (of assessed taxation)…would depend upon the value of the land disregarding any buildings or any other improvements upon it. With undeveloped land its value would reflect any potential for development…. The fundamental idea of site value presents no difficulty. It is the value of each site estimated as at the valuation date upon the assumption that any buildings or other improvements on it did not exist, but that everything surrounding it remained as it is. That is to say that the site is to be valued as if it alone were unimproved but that it enjoyed whatever advantages arise from its situation, the road system, the public services, the proximity of shops, places of entertainment, schools, churches and every other convenience of civilisation. These are in fact the advantages that have always been bought whenever a vacant site has been purchased. (1998, 65)

Current U.K. Taxes that Impinge on Land

LVT is only one form of taxation on land; others are listed by Graham (1986, 1001) as taxes that currently impinge on land in England and Wales:

- income tax and corporation tax;
- capital gains tax;
- inheritance tax;
- stamp duty;
- value added tax; and
- rates and council tax.

Income Tax and Corporation Tax

Individuals are liable to income tax, which is levied on earnings and profits at the *ad valorem* rates of 10 percent (lower rate), 22 percent (basic rate) and 40 percent (higher rate) in 2000–2001. The tax on the profits, etc., of companies is called corporation tax, which is charged at the current main rate of 30 percent, with a small companies' rate of 20 percent (dependent on level of profits).

Investment income from land. Rental profits are taxable as income under Schedule D (income and corporation taxes) and include unfurnished and furnished lettings, rent charges, way leaves, mineral royalties, tolls, premiums and woodlands. However, under Schedule A (income and corporation taxes), as Price points out, there is no charge on rents as such, but only on the profits that arise from rents and similar receipts from land (Income and Corporation Taxes Act 1988, s. 15):

> The general principle is that the profit is calculated by: (i) taking the gross amount of rent or other sum which is receivable during the year of assessment (whether or not it is actually received in that year); and (ii) deducting certain allowable expenditure which is made within the year. (1994, 4)

MacLeary (1991, 30) further specifies that the profits arising from rents and other receipts from land include rents under leases, rent charges, ground annuals, feu duties and other receipts arising as a benefit to an individual as a consequence of the ownership of an interest in land. Although rent is given its ordinary meaning, that meaning is extended to include any payments made by a tenant in the area of costs incurred in repair and maintenance, provided that such payments are also classified as rent payable under the lease. In circumstances where a premium is paid then, if the lease is granted for a period of 50 years or less, part of that premium is also treated as rent.

Trading in land. If a taxpayer is regarded as "trading in land," then the "trading profit" is taxable under Schedule D as income tax or corporation tax. The question of such trading has been the subject of judicial decisions; the position is summarised by Price:

> It seems that a person will carry on a trade if:
> (a) he buys land which is capable of producing a profit on re-sale, or he buys
>   and develops land in a manner which is capable of producing a profit;
> (b) he sells the land to one or more purchasers;
> (c) he does so for the purpose of producing a profit;
> (d) he does so recurrently or habitually; and
> (e) he does so in a commercial manner. (1994, 28)

Capital Gains Tax

When a taxpayer disposes of interest in land, that disposal may give rise to income tax liability, if the proceeds of the transaction are to be taken into account when computing trading profit. If the disposal of the interest in land does not give rise to income tax liability, the transaction will consist of the disposal of a capital asset, and, in principle, the taxpayer will have to pay a capital gains tax (CGT) on the increase in the value of the asset during the period in which the taxpayer owned it.

There is a basic distinction between income tax liability and CGT liability, but s. 98 of the Finance Act of 1988 has provided for the harmonisation of the rates of income tax and CGT. For individuals, CGT is charged at the same rates as income tax, with certain exemptions. Companies pay corporation tax at their applicable tax rates on their capital gains.

Prior to the April 1998 budget, to take account of inflation, if a disposal was made after 5 April 1982, the original cost and enhancement expenditure might be increased by indexation in proportion to the increase in the Retail Price Index from that date. However, the Finance Act of 1998 provides for indexation to be frozen from April 1998 for those within the charge to capital gains tax. The proposals will mean that for assets acquired before April 1998 and disposed of after

5 April 1998, the figures to be used for calculating the indexed rise will be as set out in a table published in May 1998. The calculation should be based on the fact that there had been a disposal in 1998. No indexation allowance will be available for any period after April 1998.

Inheritance Tax

Inheritance tax, which applies to lifetime gifts and to an estate upon death, was introduced by the Finance Act of 1986, following the abolition of capital transfer tax (CTT). Inheritance tax is based on the value of the assets owned by the taxpayer; broadly, the net value of the taxpayer's assets is known as their estate. A transfer of value is any disposition made by a person resulting in a reduction of the value of the estate. For inheritance tax purposes, each taxpayer has what might be called an "IHT history," with a principle of accumulation that is carried over to death. The tax is based on a combination of the value of taxable gifts that the taxpayer made during the last seven years of their life, and the value of the taxpayer's net worth upon death (Price 1994, 125).

The basic rules of valuation are that assets, including landed property, are to be brought into account at the price that they might reasonably be expected to fetch if sold in the open market at the time of transfer. The price is not reduced, on the ground that the market is flooded as a result of the whole of the property being notionally placed on the market at the same time. The principles, which are applied in determining the market value, are the same as those that apply for the purposes of CGT.

Stamp Duty

First imposed in 1694, the stamp duty was levied not on transactions (e.g., conveyance of landed property) themselves but on the document under which the transaction was effected. In general, ad valorem stamp duty is payable on every instrument whereby any property, or any interest in any property, is conveyed or transferred on sale (Stamp Act 1891, s. 54). However, as of 1 December 2003, stamp duty land tax (SDLT) replaces stamp duty for landed property transactions, whether or not completion takes place. (For the amount of duty, see Annexe 1.)

Value Added Tax

Value added tax (VAT) is a tax on the supply of goods and services, if the supply is a taxable supply (as defined) and made by a taxable person (as defined) in the course of that person's business. Supplying in the course of business, for VAT purposes, includes buying, selling, leasing, renting or hiring out of land or buildings on a regular basis. This could include the sale of freehold land and the sale or grant of leasehold land (exceeding 21 years), but various exemptions affect sales by builders. If applied, the full rate of VAT is currently 17.5 percent.

Rates and Council Tax

Rates and council taxes are levied on occupiers of landed property (land plus improvements and buildings) for local government revenues. In view of their special relevance to LVT, they are examined in detail in Chapter 4.

Interdependence of the Various Land Taxes

In general terms, imposing LVT affects the open market value (OMV) of land. The measure of OMV is at the heart of other land taxes, such as capital gains tax and inheritance tax. Thus, for example, if the obligation of the landowner to pay LVT reduces the OMV of that land, then other taxes that impinge on the land are consequently liable to fall.

For the purposes of this book, it is not necessary to trace through the detail of this process. However, in introducing any change in landed taxation, such interconnections between land taxes ought not to be ignored or glossed over. To date, a literature search has not revealed much detailed comment on this particular issue, but it is interesting to note Andelson on the subject.

> Obviously, some economic rent is appropriated by public authority in all countries through other means—most notably income, estate and capital gains taxes. But (with a few exceptions such as South Korea's differential levy on capital gains) in most cases it is lumped together with other returns in such a way as to defy separate identification, hence cannot be dealt with in these pages. One should note, however, that land tends to enjoy so many special tax advantages that there is reason to believe that the land-based portion of public revenue from these sources is much smaller than might otherwise be supposed. (2000, Introduction, xx)

Integrating LVT into the U.K. Tax System: Consequences of EU Membership

In later chapters, the question of how to fit LVT into the U.K. tax system will be examined in some detail, but at this stage we make the preliminary assumption that, given the political will, there should be no legal impediment to introducing LVT as either a substitute property tax or an entirely additional tax. But before considering any fundamental changes to the existing U.K. general taxation system, it is important to recognise certain aspects of the Treaty of Rome, particularly articles 95 and 100, under which the U.K. surrenders a modest part of parliamentary sovereignty to the European Union (EU). As MacLeary (1991) points out, these provisions are mainly designed to prevent discriminatory taxation between member states. More progressively, they give the EU the power to harmonise taxation between member states by the use of directives. In this way, for example, uniformity in the application of value added tax and of company taxation is being pursued. It is also true that the EU itself can raise taxes for EU revenues, which derive in part from a proportion of VAT, customs duties and agricultural levies collected in the U.K.

How far, then, and in what specific respects could the U.K.'s freedom to impose LVT be restricted by membership in the EU? Might it be necessary to get EU agreement, or uniformity of action by all EU countries, for any LVT provisions that the U.K. wished to introduce? It seems reasonably clear that, under the European treaties and directives now existing, there would be no formal restriction on U.K. freedom of action on LVT. But tax harmonisation is a controversial issue. In recent years, for example, there has been a furore over the U.K. government's refusal to accept the "withholding tax" proposal, supported by other EU member states, which is designed to harmonise taxation of savings income in the form of interest payments from direct investment.

Nevertheless, we see no specific reason why other member states should object to the introduction of LVT in the U.K. But, if it were argued that the reduction of taxes to be replaced by LVT would give the U.K. an advantage over other EU countries in investment and trade, which would be contrary to the rules of fair competition, this might become one of a set of miscellaneous issues to be horse-traded against others in some future negotiation among EU governments. Accordingly, on balance we think it right to assume at the present time that, if the U.K. government decided to introduce LVT, membership in the EU would not prevent it from doing so. Moreover, since property taxation exists in all of the countries in one form or another, LVT seems a likely candidate for investigation on harmonisation. The prospects for LVT are there, since it exists already in part within general property taxation, and the case for its retention and expansion can logically be argued (Lichfield and Connellan 2000b, 22–24).

LVT and the Prospects of Taxation Shift

In Chapter 1, we outlined the prospects of taxation shift, which included LVT and eco-taxes, and here we add a brief comment on its effect on the general tax position of the U.K. Eco-taxation follows the definition used by the European Commission (ATW Research 1996, 3), namely, that it is based on a physical unit (or proxy for it) of something that has a proven specific negative impact on the environment. It can be a tax (unrequited payments to government) or a charge (requited payments for which a service is provided by some public body generally in proportion to payment made), and these are examples of economic and financial instruments that are designed to modify market behaviour with a view to achieving government objectives (DETR 1993).

We have already suggested that introducing and enhancing these taxes could form part of a tax shift program that would radically alter the application and conception of U.K. taxes. But as we have pointed out, the U.K.'s membership in the EU may inhibit tax reform, so this aspect has to be recognised.

Summary

We have seen that certain taxes already impinge on the taxation of land (in its wider interpretation), but there are recognised difficulties in tracing the ultimate effects of such interdependence among taxes. We have also suggested that the cited definition of *land* for use with LVT would support alternative taxation (i.e., LVT combined with taxation shift) and would fit in with the overall U.K. taxation system. The wider implications of such a taxation shift have still to be considered (see Chapter 16).

■ ANNEXE ONE

Summary Description of U.K. Tax System

Income Tax

Income tax is charged on the income of individuals, partners and trusts resident in the U.K. Nonresidents deriving any income from a U.K. source must also pay income tax. The main kinds of income that are subject to this tax are earnings from employment and self-employment, unemployment benefit, pension payments during retirement, profits from business, income from property, bank and building society interest and dividends on shares.

National Insurance

Payment of national insurance contributions entitles individuals to receive certain social security benefits.

Value Added Tax (VAT)

The standard rate of value added tax in the U.K. is 17.5 percent, although since 1994–1995 there has also been a reduced rate imposed on domestic fuel, originally 8 percent but now 5 percent. Various categories of goods are either zero-rated or exempt.

Capital Taxes

Capital gains tax, introduced in 1965, is levied on gains arising from the disposal of assets by individuals, personal representatives and trustees.

Inheritance tax, introduced in 1986, replaced capital transfer tax. The tax is applied to transfers of wealth on or shortly before death that exceed a minimum threshold (£242,000 in 2001–2002 and £250,000 in 2002–2003).

Stamp duty was payable on many legal and commercial documents that transfer ownership of stock and share securities or convey landed property. Its payment is indicated by stamps on the documents, and, as of March 2000, this ranges via increasing percentages from 1 percent on transactions from £60,000/£250,000 to 4 percent for transactions over £500,000. Stamp duty is now replaced by stamp duty land tax (SDLT), since 1 December 2003, within the same percentage ranges.

Other Indirect Taxes

Excise duties are flat-rate taxes (per pint, per litre, per packet, etc.) levied upon five major goods: beer, wine, spirits, tobacco and petrol/diesel.

Vehicle excise duty is a tax on the ownership and use of vehicles; this revenue is raised through a system of annual licenses.

Insurance premium tax, which came into effect in October 1994, applies to most general insurance where the risk insured is located in the U.K.

Air passenger duty is an excise duty on air travel from U.K. airports. It came into effect on 1 November 1994.

Landfill tax, introduced in 1996, is a dual-rate tax levied on the disposal of inert and active waste at licensed landfill sites. Inert waste is subject to the lower rate of tax and active waste to the higher.

Climate change levy, which came into effect in April 2001, is charged on industrial and commercial use of electricity, coal, natural gas and liquefied petroleum, and it is aimed at reducing CO_2 emissions. The tax rate varies according to the type of fuel used.

Betting and gaming duties: General betting duty is a duty levied on the total money staked on off-course bets. Gaming duty, which replaced gaming license (premises) duty on 1 October 1997, is based on the "gross gaming yield" for each property where dutiable gaming takes place.

Corporation Tax

Corporation tax is levied on the chargeable profits of companies resident in the U.K., including public corporations and unincorporated associations. The income and chargeable gains of a company, collectively termed "chargeable profits," are chargeable to corporation tax.

Taxation of Oil Production

Petroleum revenue tax: Companies involved in the extraction of oil and gas from the U.K. and its continental shelf (mainly the North Sea) must pay petroleum revenue tax (PRT) as well as corporation tax.

Royalties: In addition to petroleum revenue tax and corporation tax, royalties are also charged on North Sea oil.

Council Tax

Properties are banded according to an assessment of their market value (as at 1 April 1991), with local authorities individually determining the rate levels levied on these bands. (See Chapter 4 for further details.)

National Nondomestic Rates

Companies pay a tax bill based on the national uniform rate poundage, being a percentage levy, on the assessed rateable value of the properties they occupy. (See Chapter 4 for further details.)

CHAPTER FOUR

Property Taxes for Local Government Revenues

B ecause current property taxes are relevant to our examination of LVT, this chapter, by Frances Plimmer, summarises the history and present application of the British rating system.

Introduction

Since 1990 Britain (England, Scotland and Wales) has had two parallel taxation systems that apply to landed property. Rates are imposed on nondomestic property; they are fixed annually by the central government, but cannot be increased above the annual rate of inflation. Rates are, however, levied, collected and spent by local authorities and therefore represent an assigned revenue. The tax is based on the net annual value of landed property and is determined as at an antecedent valuation date, currently 1 April 1998. Quinquennial revaluations are implemented and tax increases on revaluation are phased in, in accordance with a self-financing system of transitional relief.

In 1993 the community charge, or poll tax, on domestic property was replaced by a hybrid system of taxation, the council tax. Half of the tax applies to a "personal element," which assumes that two or more taxable adults are in residence; there is a reduction of 50 percent of the personal element if only one taxable adult is in occupation. If the dwelling is vacant, all of the personal element is exempt and only half of the normal tax bill is paid. The other half of the tax, the "property element," relates to the value of the property; all dwellings are allocated to one of eight value bands according to their open-market capital value as of 1 April 1991. However, to summarise the relative fiscal position: the level of council tax (on domestic property) is fixed by local authorities, but the central government retains overall control with the power to cap excessive tax-raising.

Northern Ireland retains a rates system, which is applied to the net annual value as of 2001 for nondomestic property (the Valuation List took effect in 2003 [VLA 2004]) and 1974 for domestic property. The rate is fixed, levied, collected and spent by local authorities, based on their spending programs for the forth-coming fiscal year. There are proposals to reband council tax in Wales and England, but in Northern Ireland it seems likely that a revaluation of the domestic tax base will take effect in 2006. However, in England and Wales local domestic taxation has become the subject of debate, responding to selective public pressure to reduce the level of the council tax. Dwellings have not been rebanded since the (1993) introduction of the council tax, although Wales will introduce an updated system, based on nine value bands and a valuation date of 1 April 2003 (Essex 2003), and England will introduce an updated system by 2007, although no value bands have officially been announced.

History of the Tax System

A nationwide system of property taxation was introduced in the U.K. in 1601[1] to raise revenue for welfare facilities in each parish. Over the centuries, this property tax, known as rates, evolved into an established and comprehensive system of raising income for local authority expenditure and was fixed annually by each local authority depending on its spending programme, and, after 1950, with central government (in the form of the Valuation Office Agency) providing the taxable values. Major reforms in 1990 split the system of property taxation into nondomestic and domestic property. Rates were levied only on nondomestic property—a tax whose level is determined by central government—while local authorities possess the power to levy a council tax on domestic property, although central government retains a large measure of control over the level of council tax imposed. These systems have been in operation since 1993.

The U.K. is comprised of four jurisdictions: England, Wales (which, until devolution, had the same legal and procedural systems as England), Northern Ireland (where nondomestic rating has followed a different route) and Scotland (where, because of its different legal system and devolution powers, there are variations in the process of taxing property). We assume that the system in England is similar to that of the other jurisdictions, although specific reference is also made where variations are significant in Northern Ireland, Scotland or Wales.

---

1. The Poor Relief Act of 1601, commonly known as the Statute of Elizabeth, is generally regarded as the foundation   of the present rating system, by which the "overseers" (the predecessors of the "local authority") were empowered:

   …to raise weekly or otherwise by taxation of every inhabitant parson vicar or other, and of every occupier of lands, houses, tithes impropriate or propriation of tithes, coal mines or saleable under-woods in the said parish, in such competent sums of money as they shall think fit . . . for and towards the necessary relief of the lame, impotent, old, blind, and such others among them, being poor and not able to work, and also for the putting out of such children to be apprentices. (43 Eliz. 1, c. 2)

   Although the statute imposed rating on inhabitants in respect to their real and personal estates (Sir Anthony Earby's Case 1633), in time it became the practice to disregard personal property, owing to the difficulty of ascertaining its value. Eventually the Poor Rate Exemption Act of 1840 legalised this practice, by exempting personal property and stock-in-trade from rating (Bailey et al. 1967, 2).

Property taxes are levied under the provisions of the Local Government Finance Act, 1988 (the 1988 act), which came into effect in 1990. This statute has been subsequently amended and is supplemented by several hundred statutory instruments. However, many of the principles previously established continue to apply. Thus, the legislative framework that regulates the imposition of the British property taxation system consists of statute, statutory instruments and case law. The tax levied on nondomestic property (and domestic property in Northern Ireland) is still called rates (although it was renamed the Uniform Business Rate [UBR] or National Non-Domestic Rate [NNDR] in 1990), and the tax levied on domestic property (in England, Scotland and Wales) is called council tax. Rates and council tax do not share the same legal or conceptual roots (although there are some similarities), so each is discussed separately here. However, the 1988 act ensures that, subject to specific exemption, all taxable land and buildings are subject to either rates or council tax.

Administration of Property Tax

Since its introduction in 1601, the responsibility for administering the U.K.'s property tax has shifted from the parish to local authorities or municipalities (a collection of parishes). Local authorities, therefore, are both the geographical units over which the tax is levied and also the administrative units, responsible for levying, collecting and spending the revenue. In the case of rates, the tax is fixed by the central government, but local authorities determine the level of council tax imposed on their taxpayers. Since the entire U.K. is subdivided into parishes or communities, every part of the U.K. is liable to property taxation unless exempt. In the context of levying local property taxes, local authorities are called billing authorities.

Property values for both rates and council tax are assessed by the Valuation Office Agency (VOA) (in Northern Ireland, it is called the Valuation and Land Agency [VLA], and in Scotland, the Assessors), which is an independent organisation of civil servants responsible to the central government. Valuation officers from the VOA are responsible for producing rating lists, which contain rateable (or taxable) values on which local billing authorities levy rates on nondomestic properties. These agency officers are renamed for the purposes of council tax as Listing Officers and are required to compile valuation lists containing the banded values on which the local authorities levy council tax, which is imposed in England, Scotland and Wales. Northern Ireland retains rates as a tax fixed by local authorities and imposed on both domestic and nondomestic properties.

Thus, for rates, there is an administrative split between fixing the level of rates (by the central government) and levying, collecting and spending the revenues (by the local government), but no such split exists for council tax (although the VOA fixes the taxable values for both rates and council tax). Local authorities in the U.K. have statutory responsibility for certain functions, and local authority expenditure covers education, housing, transportation, social services, police, fire and additional environmental services, such as parks maintenance and garbage collection. In order to perform these functions, the local authorities obtain their finance largely from central government grants, although in 1998–1999, 22 percent was raised from nondomestic rates (the UBR), 22 percent from council tax and 11 percent from sales, fees and charges (DETR 2000c).

Rates and council tax together represent 44 percent of local authorities' income in England. However, local authorities have direct control only over the level of council tax, subject to the central government's power to cap the level imposed if they consider it excessive. Therefore, the significance of property taxes as a source of income independent of central government control (and its implications for local democracy) is relatively limited in England, Scotland and Wales.

Rates

Rates are a tax levied on nondomestic property and the level of rate is fixed by the central government in England, Scotland and Wales. They are levied, collected and spent by local authorities. The annual rate may increase by no more than the annual level of inflation (thereby ensuring a degree of certainty over the rates bill for commercial ratepayers).

In Northern Ireland, rates retain their origins as a tax that is fixed, levied, collected and spent by local authorities, and which is applied to both domestic and nondomestic property. There is a separate rate for England, Scotland and Wales, and this rate is multiplied by the taxable (rateable) value for each nondomestic property to produce the amount of rates paid. Thus, the rate (UBR) multiplied by rateable value (RV) equals rates paid.

Rates are assessed on an annual basis, but are normally demanded and payable half-yearly in advance. Under the 1988 act, rates are a daily charge.

Taxpayer

The occupier, and not the property, is legally liable for rates (i.e., the occupier is rateable in respect of the property occupied). The nature of an occupier's liability has evolved since 1601 and has been established by case law. However, where there is no occupier, an owner may become liable to pay rates. Such an owner is required to pay half the occupied level of rates for empty properties, subject to specific exemptions.

For the purposes of establishing liability to occupied rates, there must be evidence of actual property use (actual possession); exclusion of everyone else from using the property in the same way (exclusive occupation); the property must be capable of commanding a rent (beneficial occupation); and there must be a sufficient degree of permanence (see *John Laing & Son Ltd. v Kingswood*

Assessment Committee). Thus, a vacant site or derelict building will not be liable to rates until it can be used for a valuable purpose and therefore capable of commanding a rent.

Certain taxpayers are exempt from paying rates including: those who occupy agricultural land and buildings; diplomats and those with diplomatic immunity; registered charities, who enjoy a combination of mandatory and discretionary rate relief; and other nonprofit organisations, who can apply for discretionary rate relief. Ratepayers who suffer financial hardship can also apply to the billing authority for rate relief.

Taxable Property

Legislation (s. 64 [4] 1988 Act) states that all land and buildings are rateable, unless specifically exempt. Advertising and mineral rights are also specifically mentioned as rateable property, although they are not referred to further in this text. The unit of property to be rated is called the *hereditament* (see Plimmer 1998, 37–43, for a detailed definition of hereditament) and is comprised of the land, buildings and rateable chattels.

Chattels, defined as tangible movable assets, are not normally rateable. But if they are enjoyed with land and enhance its value, they may become rateable with the land. This applies to caravans and moveable buildings such as workers quarters on a building site (see, for example, *Field Place Caravan Park Ltd. v Harding [VO]*). Items of plant and machinery are not rateable unless listed in legislation (Valuation for Rating [Plant and Machinery] Regulations, 1994). Thus, items of machinery used for providing power, heating, lighting, cooling or ventilation for a building are listed and therefore rateable as part of the land and buildings in which they are located.

A hereditament that comprises both nondomestic and domestic property, such as a shop with living accommodations, is called a composite hereditament. The occupier must pay rates on the nondomestic part and pay council tax in respect to the domestic portion of the property.

Rateable Value

Rateable value is the value ascribed to a hereditament on which rates are paid and calculated as follows: rate (UBR) multiplied by rateable value (RV) equals rates paid. Rateable value is a net annual value, specifically defined as equivalent to:

> the rent at which it is estimated the hereditament might reasonably be expected
> to let from year to year [assuming]
> (a) . . . the tenancy begins on [the] day by . . . which the determination is to be
> made;

(b) . . . the hereditament is in a state of reasonable repair, but excluding. . . any repairs which a reasonable landlord would consider uneconomic;

(c) the tenant undertakes to pay all usual tenant's rates and taxes and to bear the cost of the repairs and insurance and the other expenses (if any) necessary to maintain the hereditament in a state to command the rent. (Sch. 6 para. [2] [1]1988 Act)

The statutory definition assumes that a hypothetical tenancy exists, with a hypothetical landlord offering the hereditament for rent and a hypothetical tenant agreeing to pay the rent and undertake all repairs and other outgoings. Thus, the existence of a real tenancy or the fact that a hereditament is owner-occupied is ignored in fixing the rateable value.

The interpretation of the conditions imposed by the hypothetical tenancy, the nature of the hypothetical tenant and therefore the circumstances under which such a tenant would offer to rent the hereditament are the result of case law (see, for example, *R v Paddington [VO] ex parte Peachey Property Corporation Ltd.*; see also Plimmer 1998, 59–70). For example, when assessing the rateable value of a hereditament, it is assumed that the property is vacant and for rent; it is valued *rebus sic stantibus* (as is), provided that no changes are made in the mode of use or in the physical structure (with the exception of the state of repair, because rateable value assumes that the hypothetical landlord will put the property into good repair at the start of the tenancy and that the hypothetical tenant will observe the repairing covenant). Rates, therefore, tax the value of the property in its existing use and ignore any other potential use until it occurs.

Antecedent Valuation Date

Since 1990 all nondomestic hereditaments in England, Scotland and Wales are subject to quinquennial revaluations; the latest revaluation in England and Wales, which took effect on 1 April 2000, has an antecedent valuation date of 1 April 1998. Thus, the VOA revalued all nondomestic hereditaments in their physical state as of 1 April 2000, but at the level of value (or tone of the list) that existed on the antecedent valuation date of 1 April 1998. The use of such an antecedent valuation date permits the VOA to gather market evidence around that date, analyse it, establish an appropriate level of values, undertake the process of valuing all hereditaments, and pass the resulting rateable values to the billing authorities so that they can issue the rates demands by 1 April 2000. Thus, a greater degree of valuation accuracy is achieved and fewer appeals result.

It follows that all properties to be taxed between 1 April 2000 and 1 April 2005 (when the next revaluation takes effect) must be valued as at the antecedent valuation date of 1 April 1998. (Unlike the rest of the U.K., Northern Ireland has a nondomestic tax base that took effect in 2003 with a valuation date of 1974.)

Methods of Valuation

There is no legal requirement to use any particular method of valuation for rating purposes, although certain specified operational hereditaments, normally occupied by providers of utilities such as gas, electricity and water, are valued using a statutory formula.

Since it is necessary to establish a rateable value (i.e., a net annual value) for each hereditament, open-market rents, fixed at or near the valuation date, are considered to be the best method of valuation. The VOA has statutory power to require owners and occupiers of hereditaments to provide details of rents paid, so that rateable values of hereditaments can be assessed. For certain property types, however, rental evidence is not available and even where such evidence is available, it may provide unsuitable or unreliable information for establishing a rateable value. There is, therefore, widespread use of a profits (expenditure and receipts) method and a cost-based approach (or Contractor's Basis) for fixing rateable values where the use of rental evidence is not appropriate (see, for example, Plimmer 1998, 72–116; and Scarrett 1991).

Regardless of the method of valuation adopted, it is important to establish a rent that a hypothetical tenant would pay for the hereditament as at the valuation date. For any method of valuation, it is necessary to ensure that it conforms to the terms and interpretation of the hypothetical tenancy according to the definition of rateable value and other conditions imposed by the rating law.

In valuing an office hereditament, for example, typically one investigates the open-market rental value (as at the antecedent valuation date) of the hereditament (the land, buildings and rateable plant and machinery) in its current state, based on: the rent paid by the actual occupier (if any); and the rent paid by occupiers of comparable hereditaments in the locality, making appropriate allowances for material differences in both the hereditaments and location.

Rating Lists

All rateable values are contained in local nondomestic rating lists—one list for each billing authority area. Rateable values for utilities such as gas, electricity and water are contained in a central rating list. It is the duty (s. 41 [1] 1988 Act) of the Valuation Officer to compile and then maintain a local nondomestic rating list comprising all relevant nondomestic and composite hereditaments for each local or billing authority.

The contents of the rating lists must comply with certain regulations (s. 42 [2] 1988 Act). Billing authorities hold copies of the local rating lists and demand rates are sent out based on the list entries. When an entry requires amendment, the VOA informs the billing authority, which makes the appropriate change to its copy. The rating lists are conclusive proof of rate liability (ss. 43 [1] and 45 [1] 1988 Act). Hereditaments that are entirely exempt are not valued and are excluded from the list, although composite hereditaments are included in the list and are identified as composite.

Since 1990 each new revaluation (in 1990, 1995 and 2000) has been accompanied by a self-financing system of transitional relief that allows for the phasing in of both increases and decreases in rate liability. Transitional relief is justified to protect businesses against sudden and dramatic increases in their rates bills. However, the central government requires that such transitional relief be self-funding. Thus, the occupiers of those nondomestic hereditaments whose rateable values have increased by a certain percentage on revaluation have their increased rates phased in over a period of years; while the occupiers of those nondomestic hereditaments whose rateable values have decreased will see their reduced rates phased in at a level that pays for the increases.

Appeals

Appeals for ratepayers are possible against the rate level (UBR) fixed by the central government by way of judicial review, but, more usually, ratepayers challenge the rateable value by proposing an amendment to the rating list. Such a proposal can be made by any interested person (such as an occupier or owner), although the Valuation Officer can alter the list without making a proposal. The procedure for dealing with appeals is complex and contains statutory instruments (Non-Domestic Rating [Alteration of Lists and Appeals] Regulations [as amended]).

Valuation Tribunals, the courts that first hear appeals against valid proposals, are able to determine the correct rateable value and the effective date of any amendment to rating list entries. Appeals to the Valuation Tribunals are relatively inexpensive, quick and easy for ratepayers.[2]

An appeal against the decision of the Valuation Tribunal is made to the Lands Tribunal and then, on a point of law only, to the Court of Appeal and thereafter to the House of Lords. Any determination of a point of law that affects the valuation is referred back to the Lands Tribunal, which is the highest court for the determination of valuation issues.

Rate Collection and Recovery

Billing authorities collect rates in their area. Rates are sought half-yearly in advance, although they can be paid in ten monthly instalments. If they are not paid in full, the billing authority can apply to the magistrates' court for a liability order, under which goods can be seized from the premises of the defaulting rate-

---

2. See Valuation and Community Charge Tribunals (Transfer of Jurisdiction) Regulations 1989 (SI 1989 no. 440) and s. 15 of Local Government Finance Act, 1992; and Plimmer 1998, 140–149, for additional details of powers and procedures.

payer and sold to cover the outstanding debt. Other remedies include committal to prison and insolvency. There is an appeal to the High Court by anyone aggrieved against the decision of the magistrates' court.

Council Tax

In 1990, when the Uniform Business Rate was introduced in England and Wales, the previous system of taxation of domestic property was replaced by a flat rate community charge (or poll tax) that was fixed, levied, administered and spent by the local authorities. The community charge (or poll tax) had been initiated in Scotland in the previous year. However, the introduction of this system resulted in civil unrest, and within eight months of its introduction in England and Wales, the British government was devising its replacement (for a critique, see Plimmer 1998, 195–205; Plimmer et al. 2000a and 2000b).

The council tax was introduced in England, Scotland and Wales on 1 April 1993 (in the Local Government Finance Act, 1992) and is, effectively, a hybrid property tax and poll tax; half of the tax assumes that there are two taxable adults residing in the dwelling and the other half relates to the banded value of the property. The tax is fixed, levied, administered, collected and spent by local (billing) authorities but central government retains the power to cap local authority spending, effectively controlling the level of council tax that the municipalities can impose. Although a very new system in principle, the council tax retains many similarities to rates, both in definition and practice. The community charge had been incurred on a daily basis and the 1990 system of rates was introduced to match this liability. Its replacement, the council tax, also involves a daily liability, although in both systems bills are normally paid annually or monthly.

Taxpayer

Liability to pay the council tax belongs primarily to the occupier, although the Local Government Finance Act of 1992 imposes a hierarchy of liability. Those residents with a legal interest in the property are the first called upon to pay; followed by residents with no legal interest in the property; and finally an owner of a dwelling in which there is no resident at all. Thus, as with rates, the council tax is initially an occupier's tax, with an owner being responsible to pay (only the property element) if there is no occupier, although there are certain exemptions from council tax.

Half the normal level of council tax is paid on second homes. However, in November 2002, the government announced that under legislation that will go through Parliament in 2003, councils in England and Wales will be allowed to set their own level of discount for second-home owners, on a sliding scale of 10–50 percent.

Personal Element

Reflecting its community charge origin, the council tax bill assumes that there are two taxable adults residing in a dwelling. A relief of 50 percent of half the bill (25 percent of the entire bill) is given if there is only one taxable adult resident, and a relief of 100 percent of this amount (50 percent of the entire bill) is given if there is no taxable adult residing in the dwelling. However, no additional tax is charged if there are more than two taxable adults living in the dwelling.

This tax relief applied to the personal element reflects the reluctance of the British government in 1991 to abandon entirely the poll tax principles, and is applied regardless of the value of the property or of the financial circumstances of the occupier. Residents who are considered exempt include persons in detention (subject to certain conditions); severely mentally impaired people; and students. A system of benefits has been incorporated into the social security legislation, so that low-income residents are entitled to tax rebates of up to 100 percent.

Property Element

Domestic property, which was specifically excluded from the definition of hereditament for rating purposes, is liable to council tax. For both taxes, the definition of domestic property is the same (s. 66 [1] 1988 Act), that is, "property [that is] used wholly for the purposes of living accommodation," which includes a private garage, private storage premises, mooring and caravan pitch used for private dwellings. The criteria that such a dwelling must also be hereditament is retained (for a definition of hereditament, see Plimmer 1998, 30–43, 176–178).

Certain hereditaments are exempt from council tax, including vacant dwellings that are undergoing structural or other major works to render them habitable; dwellings that have been vacant for less than six months; and unoccupied dwellings where habitation is prohibited (Council Tax [Exempt Dwellings] Order, 1992).

Basis of Valuation

For the purposes of council tax, the value of any dwelling is defined as "the amount which, on the assumptions mentioned . . . below, the dwelling might reasonably be expected to realise if it had been sold in the open market by a willing vendor on the 1st April 1991" (para. 6 [1] of the Council Tax [Situation and Valuation of Dwellings] Regulations, 1992).

Among the assumptions are: the sale was with vacant possession; the size, layout and character of the dwelling and the physical state of the locality were the same as on the date the valuation was made; the dwelling was in reasonable repair; and the dwelling had no development value other than that attributed to the permitted development. Thus, the value on which council tax is levied is the capital value of the dwelling, as at the antecedent valuation date of 1 April 1991, assuming existing use.

Strictly speaking, however, dwellings are not "valued" for the purposes of council tax. Each dwelling is merely allocated to one of eight value bands, based on the definition of valuation cited above. The value bands vary, with one set applied to England and Scotland, and a different set applied to Wales (see Tables 2 and 3). The value bands were determined by the average property values in each country, and the central government has the power to vary the values within the bands and to substitute other value bands for those currently in force.

In addition to applying bands to properties, the central government controls the level of taxation relative to the different bands. Thus, the tax fixed for the so-called average Band D is half that levied on the highest value Band H properties; and is 50 percent greater than that levied on lowest value Band A properties. The relativities imposed are demonstrated in Table 4.

The numbers represent the relative proportions of the council tax bill that are paid by council tax payers whose properties fall within the different bands. For example, if a particular local authority set a council tax level of £500 for

TABLE 2 Council Tax Bands for England and Scotland

Valuation Band	Range of Values
A	Not exceeding £40,000
B	Exceeding £40,000 but not exceeding £52,000
C	Exceeding £52,000 but not exceeding £68,000
D	Exceeding £68,000 but not exceeding £88,000
E	Exceeding £88,000 but not exceeding £120,000
F	Exceeding £120,000 but not exceeding £160,000
G	Exceeding £160,000 but not exceeding £320,000
H	Exceeding £320,000

TABLE 3 Council Tax Bands for Wales

Valuation Band	Range of Values
A	Not exceeding £30,000
B	Exceeding £30,000 but not exceeding £39,000
C	Exceeding £39,000 but not exceeding £51,000
D	Exceeding £51,000 but not exceeding £66,000
E	Exceeding £66,000 but not exceeding £90,000
F	Exceeding £90,000 but not exceeding £120,000
G	Exceeding £120,000 but not exceeding £240,000
H	Exceeding £240,000

TABLE 4 Relativity of Council Tax Liability							
Band A	Band B	Band C	Band D	Band E	Band F	Band G	Band H
6	7	8	9	11	13	15	18

properties in Band D, owners of properties in Band A would pay (6/9 x £500)=£333; those in Band D would pay (9/9 x £500)=£500; and those in Band H would pay (18/9 x £500) =£1,000.

Since they were introduced in 1993, there has been no review of the value bands, nor has there been a revaluation or rebanding of properties. Thus, the council tax is levied on the tax base that was established on 1 April 1993, with a valuation date of 1 April 1991. There is now a proposal to reband in 2005 in Wales (Essex 2003) and in 2007 in England.[3]

Methods of Valuation

Council tax is based on the capital value of dwellings, as of 1 April 1991. The method of valuation used is, therefore, based on direct comparable market transactions. However, since it is not necessary to make a discrete valuation for each dwelling, but merely to allocate them to an appropriate value band, the level of valuation skill, the speed and cost with which the valuation exercise can be undertaken, and the amount of comparable market evidence required are less than that required to provide a discrete taxable value (as is required for a nondomestic hereditament).

Valuation Lists

All taxable domestic hereditaments in each local billing authority area are entered into a valuation list. The Valuation Officer (renamed the Listing Officer for the purposes of the council tax) is required to compile and maintain a valuation list for each local authority area. The contents of the valuation lists must comply with regulations (Council Tax [Contents of Valuation Lists] Regulations, 1992).

---

3. The last revaluation of hereditaments (subject to rates) was in 2000, with the next scheduled for 2005, as part of an established quinquennial review pattern. Originally, the British government had no plan to revalue or reband nondomestic property (the banding system was considered to obviate the need for such a review), but in 2001 the U.K. government proposed a 10-year revaluation cycle for the council tax, with new valuation lists for England taking effect in 2007 based on valuations as of 2005 (DLTR 2001, 1). Wales is proposing an eight-year revaluation cycle (Essex 2003). Despite this proposal, such a timetable means that the current lists in England will have lasted for 14 years, based on valuations up to 16 years old, with the probability that the rebanding exercise will result in taxpayer protests. There is a commitment to ensuring that such a rebanding exercise will not lead to any overall change in yield and to "ensure that the council tax burden is distributed fairly on the basis of more up-to-date property values" (DLTR 2001, 1; Essex 2003). There remains, however, the danger that some form of transitional relief will be introduced (as for nondomestic taxpayers after a revaluation) to prevent any relatively large increases in liability. Again, based on the nondomestic experience, such a relief will likely be self-financing, thereby totally removing the effect that a revaluation or rebanding exercise is designed to achieve.

A copy of the list is held by the billing authorities, who send out council tax demands based on the entries.

Appeals

Appeals against council tax liability and against a dwelling's band assignment are made to the Valuation Tribunal (Council Tax [Alteration of Lists and Appeals] Regulations, 1993). Interested persons (an owner or occupier) have only limited rights in proposing any changes to valuation list.

Summary

Viewing the British property tax system within the context of the general taxation system, it seems that there is no major conceptual impediment to introducing LVT as a replacement tax for either the UBR or the council tax (or even as an additional tax); LVT could be reasonably accommodated within the extant general taxation system. In the next chapter, we assess further the possibility of introducing LVT by examining the history of previous attempts at imposing this form of taxation in Britain.

CHAPTER FIVE

History of Attempts at Land Value Taxation in Britain

This chapter examines the ways LVT (mainly in the form of site value rating [SVR] as an ongoing tax) has been attempted throughout Britain's history. Note that here we are addressing the tax in its simplest form: the process of raising an annual tax on land values, usually to meet some elements of government expenditures.[1]

Background

A quotation from the journal of the Land Value Tax Campaign stresses the philosophical (and even theological) arguments for regarding land as a common, not privately owned, resource:

> Definition of the rights of ownership and of property determines the relationship of citizens to each other, and of the citizen to the state. Whether there was a Divine Creator or not, the Earth was certainly not made by man. It follows that all men have equal rights in the bounty of Nature. A man may not own what neither he nor any other man created. It is the exertion of labour which confers legitimacy on a claim to ownership. Those who would guide public morals must not think they may shrink from a stand on an issue of such fundamental significance. The Earth, we think, is not Caesar's to dispose of. (1996, 1)

Despite this exposition of apparent natural law, however latterly expressed, the Romans were not averse to codifying a complex system of property jurisprudence, at the heart of which the control, transfer and ownership of rights over land were clearly evident (Gibbon 1951, vol. 4, 419–429). The Romans also recognised land as a target for measurement and assessment by surveyors for taxation on a quinquennial basis (Gibbon 1951, vol. 2, 124), and this would have been a normal part of imperial taxation in Roman Britain during the four centuries of occupation in the first millennium. But even the Romans were

---

1. Other forms of LVT, such as recoupment via ownership, development value capture and recovery of infrastructure costs, are covered in subsequent chapters.

following an earlier tradition of land taxation, as evidenced in Persia, Egypt and the Maurayan Empire in India in 300 B.C., where two types of taxes were levied, one on the amount of land cultivated and the other on the produce of the land (*Encyclopaedia Britannica* 1997, vol. 21, 41).

However, in Britain there was no systematic appraisal of supporting rationales for land taxation per se until the nineteenth century, although pragmatically various earlier attempts were made to levy special taxes on land. For example, in 1604 Robert Cecil, Earl of Salisbury, examined proposals to commute certain fiscal rights into an annual sum to be raised by a land tax. By 1610 there had been some progress, but the government eventually backed down, believing the sum was too low; the leaders of the Commons also thought that a land tax would be too unpopular (*Encyclopaedia Britannica* 1997, vol. 29, 55).

From Britain's past, Wilks summarised the fleeting remnants of land taxation by confirming, "One or two very minor residual taxes based on the value of bare land still existed; these were known as Danegeld, land tax and Queen Anne's Bounty . . . for all practical purposes, these taxes, the residue of a system that was in force 700 or more years ago, could be forgotten" (1975, 1). The basic arguments for LVT were extensively debated in political and economic circles in Britain from the latter part of the nineteenth century, and, from that time up through 1939, municipal authorities made many attempts to persuade Parliament to allow them to levy rates on land values (see Table 5 and Annexe 2 to this chapter). None succeeded.

In addition, central government did attempt to introduce land value duties as taxation for national and local purposes in 1910 and again in 1931. Although enacted, these measures proved unworkable and unacceptable in practice, and they were eventually abandoned before they could be fully implemented. But the pressure to introduce some form of LVT did not abate, and in 1942 and 1952 two government-appointed committees (Uthwatt and Simes) reported findings relevant to the possible introduction of LVT.

Interest in LVT During and After World War II

In the period during and immediately following World War II, many interested parties wished to investigate further the possibility of introducing LVT. We now examine the findings of two important committees appointed to review these matters.

Uthwatt Committee (1942)

The Uthwatt Committee, which reported on the compensation and betterment problem (see also Chapter 7), positively recommended a form of LVT in its proposal for a levy on enhanced annual site values as a practical method of recouping betterment (Uthwatt 1942, 154). The levy was to run alongside the existing rating system; in the valuation lists made for rating purposes, it was proposed that there be an additional column containing the quinquennially measured annual site value of every hereditament separately assessable for rates.

Uthwatt also trailed the further possibility of linking the collection of local government revenues with the recoupment of betterment by suggesting that ascertaining annual site values would also provide a basis for the differential rating of sites and buildings to the relief of improvements, should it be desired to introduce such a system. (This prospect is covered further in Chapter 10.)

Very little comment on this proposal can be gleaned from later examinations of the prospects of LVT, although a brief reference appeared in the report of the Simes Committee (1952, 25), but without any evaluation of its possibilities. The solution it proposed was never tried.

Simes Committee (1947–1952)

Later, in 1947, the government appointed a committee of enquiry under the chairmanship of Erskine Simes "to consider and report on the practicability and desirability of meeting part of local expenditure by an additional rate on site values, having regard to the provisions of the Town and Country Planning Acts and other factors" (Simes 1952, 4).

It was subsequently confirmed that:

- the words "additional rate on site values" meant a rate levied upon a separate assessment of site values; and
- the expression "site values" included site values of agricultural land. (Simes 1952, 4)

The Simes Committee reported after four and a half years, in 1952, when the development charge provisions of the Town and Country Planning Act of 1947 were in operation (see also Chapter 7). This cramped the committee's scope, since in its terms of reference it needed to have regard to this act. The committee had a difficult task: figuring out how to assess the development charge on a property if that property's development rights were shared by both the landowner (who had pre-1947 development rights) and the government (which could impose a development charge corresponding to the increased development value at the later date of the planning applications). This and other considerations led the majority of the committee (six members) to reject LVT, but a minority (three members) dissented.

The committee also recorded in some detail the history of material relevant to the taxation of site values, which we have referred to above. (See Table 5, derived from the committee's summary of the legislative proposals for the introduction of LVT in Britain up to 1939. Further details of the main legislative attempts are provided in Annexe 2 to this chapter.)

TABLE 5 History of Attempts to Introduce Land Value Taxation in Britain from the Late Nineteenth Century to World War II

Derived from a Schedule of Legislative Proposals (Original Source: Simes Committee Report 1952)

Proposal	To Meet Local Expenses	Levied on Annual or Capital Value	Limitation on Amount of Rate	Outcome
Royal Commission on Housing of Working Classes, 1885	Part	-	-	Commission accepted argument that LVT (or SVR) would increase the supply of land available for housing and recommended future legislation.
LCC Evidence to Royal Commission on Local Taxation, 1899	Part	Capital	6d. in £. (2.5%)	LCC (London County Council) considered that owners should be rated on the basis of site value, as later embodied in LCC 1901 Bill.
"Separate Report" of Royal Commission on Local Taxation, 1901	Part	Annual	To be fixed by Parliament	Proposed that a site value rate should be charged half on owners and half on occupiers—initially in urban areas alone. These proposals formed the basis of several private bills submitted in 1902–1905.
Judge O'Connor's Minority Report (Royal Commission on Local Taxation), 1901	Whole	-	-	Advised that the rating of site values to meet the cost of all public services was practicable.
LCC Bill, 1901	Part	Annual	2s. in £ (10%)	Followed the LCC evidence to the Royal Commission 1901 and was subsequently presented to Parliament but not approved.
Mr. C.P. Trevelyan's Bill, 1902	Part	Annual	2s. in £ (10%)	Private bill, influenced by "minority report" of Royal Commission 1901, but not subsequently approved by Parliament.
Dr. T.J. MacNamara's Bill, 1903	Part	Capital	1d. in £ (0.42%)	Private bill, influenced by "minority report" of Royal Commission 1901, but not subsequently approved by Parliament.

Bill	Whole or Part	Basis	Rate	Remarks
Mr. C.P. Trevelyan's Bill, 1904, and Sir John Brunner's Bill, 1905	Part	Annual, defined as 3% of capital value	Same rate on improved value of occupied land and unimproved value of unoccupied land	Private bills, influenced by "minority report" of Royal Commission 1901, but not subsequently approved by Parliament.
Land Values Taxation (Scotland) Bill, 1905	Part	Annual, defined as 4% of capital value	2s. in £ (10%)	Bill passed its second reading in Parliament, but was then referred to a select committee for further consideration (see below).
Select Committee on Land Values Taxation (Scotland) Bill, 1906	Whole	Annual	-	Approved the principle of rating site values in the 1905 bill, but required changes to be incorporated in the Land Values (Scotland) Bill (1907). This later bill was not passed by the House of Lords and was thus abandoned.
Finance (1909–1910) Act and Land Value Duties Act, 1910	Part proposed but eventually undetermined	Capital Capital	Incremental and reversionary duties (10%). Annual levy on undeveloped land (0.21%)	These acts, as applied to land value taxation, proved unworkable in practice and nonproductive in revenue. The measures were eventually repealed by Finance Act of 1920.
Departmental Committee on Local Taxation, 1914 (Minority Report)	Part	Capital	10% of amount raised in rates plus half of any future increases	Minority report of this committee accepted the separate report of the Royal Commission 1901 and recommended site value rates for both urban and rural areas. Majority report recommended against any rate on site values.
Manchester Bill, 1921	Part	Annual, defined as 5% of capital value	-	Local authority bill, presented to Parliament but not approved.
Finance Act, 1931	-	Capital	1d. in £ (0.42%) originally proposed	Taxation of land values for "national purposes" was approved by the passing of this act but suspended following change of government in 1932 and finally repealed by the Finance Act of 1934.
Mr. J.C. (later Lord) Wedgwood's Bill, 1932	Whole or Part	Capital	-	Private member's bill, presented to Parliament but not approved.
Mr. A. MacLaren's Bill, 1937	-	Annual	-	Private member's bill, presented to Parliament but not approved.
L.C.C. Bill, 1938–1939	Part	Annual	2s. in £ (10%)	Local authority bill, presented to Parliament but not approved.

Simes reported the findings of the committee as follows:

Majority Report:

> We may summarise our findings by saying that insofar as we have been impressed by the historical case for the rating of site values, we are nevertheless of the opinion that this historical case and the evidence from overseas is not relevant to the conditions in Great Britain today.
>
> We consider that the impact of the Town and Country Planning Act, 1947, has altered the position by enforcing the claims of the community to the fruits of development of land as far as they can be foreseen. We do not deny the possibility of the rating of site values, but we have been impressed with the administrative difficulties, the prospect of litigation which would inevitably arise, the undesirability diverting much-needed manpower for the purpose and the relatively small revenue likely to be obtained and can find no significant advantages in its introduction.
>
> We accordingly report that the meeting of any part of local expenditure by an additional rate on site values, having regard to the Town and Country Planning Act and other relevant factors, is neither practicable nor desirable. (Simes 1952, 76)

Minority Report:

> - The rating of site values is both practical and desirable. The arguments in favour of it stand unimpaired.
> - The only event since 1939 having a material bearing upon the matter is the Town and Country Planning Act, 1947. This involves some changes in the method of application but does not affect the principle.
> - Local authorities should be required to raise a minimum rate in the pound on site values, and should be empowered to raise a higher rate if they think fit.
> - Valuations of site value should be made by the Valuation Office of the Department of Inland Revenue.
> - Valuation Lists should be open to inspection by the public.
> - Scientific methods of valuation should be employed (e.g., in urban areas, land value maps).
> - Objections to valuation should be dealt with so as to ensure a uniformity of valuation, and the tribunal dealing with them should be both expert in matters of valuation and familiar with values in the district affected. (Simes 1952, 76)

The Minority recommendations went on to include:

> To deal with quinquennial re-valuations, that the primary valuation should be of the unrestricted site value, and this site value should be estimated as an annual site value (i.e., the yearly rent which might be expected to yield if let at the valuation date upon a perpetual tenure). Furthermore where the ownership of land is divided between several interests, each should bear its appropriate share of the site value rate by a system of deduction from rent. Furthermore the rating of site

values should apply to agricultural land and other de-rated hereditaments. The exemption from local rates given to buildings occupied for certain religious or scientific purposes should not extend to exonerate from site value rate those who received rents from such occupiers. (Simes 1952, 98)

Subsequent Investigations

After 1952, with various changes in government, the whole financial provisions affecting development value arising from the 1947 Planning Act were under review and in process of fundamental changes (these are described in Chapter 7). However, partly because of these changes, there was still a continuing consideration of the prospects of LVT from professional bodies and later from a government-appointed committee and a government green paper and other enquiries, which are summarised below.

Royal Institute of Public Administration (1956)

The RIPA's report examined possible new sources of local revenue and gave an account of the operation of LVT in other countries, stating that where it had been adopted it appeared to be successful. However, the report concluded that while the argument for LVT, which encourages the development of land, is a particularly useful tax in an expanding country with a large area of land, it is of less interest in a country like Great Britain.

Blundell commented on this finding:

> That Britain has a relatively small area of land makes it more, not less, necessary, to ensure that the land which is available for expansion is not left idle or underdeveloped, whilst making no contribution to the local services which help maintain and raise its value. (1993, 18)

Whitstable Surveys: Hector M. Wilks (1964, 1974, 1975)

Originally this was a commissioned survey of a town in Kent (Whitstable), which in 1963 tested the practicalities and effects of introducing LVT as an alternative to the established rating of landed property as combined hereditaments of land and buildings. The survey was conducted by H.M. Wilks, a leading rating surveyor, who adopted the LCC Bill's definitions of site value. He concluded that the exercise was professionally feasible but that it inevitably shifted the burden of rates between different types of property.

In 1973 Wilks revalued Whitstable with an amended definition of annual site value, and reflecting on this second valuation, he confirmed:

> Comparability with the orthodox method—the total rateable value is of the same order as the orthodox rateable value list, because of the extra land and so on that one brings in and the extra values that accrue, so that the rate poundage can be of the same order of figure. It is clear and incisive to operate and from the valuer's

point of view, the number of problems seems to be far less than those which we have to meet on the orthodox system.

The only problem that I can see in this country in bringing in such a method is the interim period or changeover. It is so bound into the system in this country that the occupier pays the rates. All leases of and transactions in land are based on this premise. Is it worth upsetting all this, is it worth having to review by statute every transaction in land, every lease of land for this other system of taxation? Now that I have done my two reports my answer is an uncompromising "Yes." It is all worthwhile. (1975, 11–12)

It is also worth recording the forthright opinions of Wilks (1975, 10–11) when he reflects on his second pilot survey for LVT at Whitstable[4] and the ability of landowners to pay such taxes. His clear view was that the ratepayers own the land out of which the tax emanates, and it is up to them to see that the land is developed to its optimum so that they are able to pay the annual impost. If they do not, only they are to blame. He regarded the assessment of annual site values as a more practical and ready process than the extant statutory valuation basis of combined hereditaments of land and buildings. As to the suitability of the tax for producing revenue, Wilks was equally forthright in confirming that the general rate at the time was held to be one of the most easily collected taxes and was cheap to administer, but that under LVT there would be fewer taxpayers, easier recovery and even lower costs.

Royal Institution of Chartered Surveyors (1964)

The Royal Institution of Chartered Surveyors in 1964 set up a working party to examine, among other things, whether anything had changed after the demise of the compensation/betterment provisions of the Town and Country Planning Act of 1947. It essentially came to the same conclusion as the Simes Committee in 1952.

> The majority report of the Erskine Simes Committee (1952) came to the conclusion that site value rating was neither practicable nor desirable. We have endeavoured to look again at the problem, bearing in mind that development charges introduced by the Town and Country Planning Act, 1947 have been abolished, and by taking into account the information made available by the Whitstable Pilot Survey we have come to the same conclusion. (RICS 1964, 14)

---

4. The Lincoln Institute of Land Policy awarded David C. Lincoln Fellowships for 2002–2003 and 2003–2004 to Frances Plimmer and Greg McGill to examine the effects of LVT in the U.K., updating the Whitstable case studies originally carried out by Wilks in 1963 and 1973. The aim of this project is to again focus on Whitstable and to establish site and property values for all the taxable units (hereditaments) in the town, taking into account the methodology used in 1973 and more recent advances in valuation, appraisal methods and geographic information systems.

Ministry of Housing and Local Government (1971)

A 1971 green paper from the Ministry of Housing and Local Government considered trends in local government expenditure, possible additional sources of revenue, improvements of the rating system, and the future system of control of government grants. Various options were examined but none specifically recommended. As far as its consideration of site value rating, Blundell (1993, 19) opined "In the examination of SVR, there is little evidence of original thinking, and the misconceptions of the Simes report were repeated without further consideration."[5]

Layfield Committee (1976)

The Layfield Report, a 1976 report on Local Government Finance from another government-appointed committee, examined various taxation options, including LVT, for providing local government revenues. The report rejected LVT and favoured retaining the existing rating system; in this way it was influenced by the Development Land Tax Act 1976 (see Chapter 7). However, the report recommended that domestic dwellings be assessed on capital values rather than on annual values because there was more evidence of the former than of the latter. It further recommended that agricultural land and buildings should be rated and that a local income tax should be levied as an additional source of revenue.

Layfield concluded that the proposed development land tax and the Community Land Act effectively remove site value rating from consideration. Apart from these developments, a tax on site values was not considered to be a suitable or a firm enough base for raising local revenue. Local accountability would not be promoted. The practical difficulties are formidable. At least a decade would be necessary to put site value rating into use, with a long period of transition thereafter before it could become fully operative. (Layfield 1976, Annexe 21)

V. H. Blundell's Findings on LVT

Blundell provides a close analysis of the findings of the Simes Committee:

> Although the Committee acknowledged the force of much evidence in favour of SVR, it repeatedly came up against the instruction that it should have regard to the financial provision of the 1947 [Planning] Act—which effectively nullified the value of this evidence. The minority report attempted, without much difficulty, to reconcile SVR with the 1947 Act, and indeed a case of a kind was made out. But with the practical difficulties involved, the case was hardly likely to seem wholly convincing. (1993, 16)

---

5. For a further discussion of these misconceptions, see Chapter 7.

But it is also interesting and pertinent to quote Blundell's findings on the outcome of the various enquiry committees into LVT over the later period, 1952–1976, as he encapsulates the fundamental issues in his conclusion:

> During the period when these various enquiry committees have sat to consider site value rating, one or other of a succession of land reform Acts was in operation. These Acts were alleged either to inhibit the introduction of SVR (Site Value Rating), or already to be serving its main purpose. **The confusion of a development tax with an ad valorem tax on all land values has persisted throughout.**[6] However, the financial provisions of these Acts have long been repealed, and therefore those objections to SVR which were based upon them are no longer relevant.
>
> The two Whitstable valuations by Wilks, H. M. (1964, 1974, 1975) have shown that most of the other criticisms were unfounded. Despite conclusive evidence to the contrary, opponents of SVR continue to claim that the Whitstable site valuations would have "priced amenities out of existence," and to quote the Simes Report as though nothing had happened since. (1993, 22)

More Recent Commentaries

It is salutary that although there was a decline in officially inspired comment on LVT after the 1970s, there has nevertheless been considerable renewed attention to this form of taxation over recent years.

The Urban Task Force, set up in 1998 by the deputy prime minister to report on policies for urban renewal, recommended a vacant land tax (VLT), levied annually, as one highly effective measure to stimulate urban renewal, and it also called for further studies of "mixed model site value rating":

> Thinking about the longer term, and in view of the growing requirement and expectation to recognize the value of land as a finite environmental resource, there is the more fundamental issue of whether our current system of commercial property taxation the Uniform Business Rate is the best system to help us manage our scarce land and buildings resources over the first half of the next century. We are not the first to consider this question. The Layfield Committee Report on Local Government Finance [Layfield 1976] considered the merits of site value rating back in 1976 and concluded "the practical difficulties would be formidable." Nevertheless, experience overseas suggests that it may be time for a re-consideration. A mixed rating model could provide us with an alternative way forward. This is, however, a question for others to consider in more detail. (Rogers et al. 1999)

A report by the Fabian Society, a left-wing think tank, contains a whole chapter on LVT (Plant Commission 2000, chap. 14). Although it concludes that "today land taxation is more sensibly viewed as a form of environmental taxation" (Plant Commission 2000, 318), the report implies that LVT would not work

---

6. Author's bolding; this confusion is further commented upon in Chapter 1.

alongside the British planning system—but it does not clearly explain why. However, the report reserves judgment on such practicalities and recommends a range of pilots of Pennsylvania-style SVR, being a dual-rate basis on separate assessments of land and buildings. After looking at a proposal to introduce LVT "by splitting business rates into an owner's and an occupier's component," which "has been introduced successfully elsewhere," it recommends "establishment of pilot schemes in different local authority areas of two-tier business rates; to investigate their feasibility and effectiveness in the U.K. context" (Plant Commission 2000, 13, 319; see also Chapter 15 and Appendix E).

Scottish Office Land Reform Policy Group

After enumerating more "advantages" for LVT in its *Identifying the Solutions* report (September 1998) than for any of its other 64 policy proposals, this group included in *Recommendations for Action* (January 1999) a comprehensive economic evaluation of the possible impact of moving in the longer term to a LVT basis. The Scottish Rating and Valuation Council is now considering a report by the Scottish executive on what further LVT research might represent value for money, prior to making recommendations to the first minister. In January 2001 the local government committee of the Scottish Parliament also specifically took evidence on LVT in its inquiry into local government finance.

Report for Town & Country Planning Association (TCPA)

Following the Urban Task Force report, TCPA was funded by Joseph Rowntree Foundation to commission a series of roundtable discussions by experts on the fiscal options for achieving urban renewal. Bob Evans of South Bank University and Richard Bate, standing adviser to the House of Commons Environment Committee, included as one of their recommendations: "The Government should seriously examine the case for establishing a system of land value taxation in the longer term" (Evans and Bate 2000, 1–2).

Consolidated Findings

What emerges from a study of these events is that, despite the strength of social, economic and political pressures since the late nineteenth century, successive governments have had a distinct lack of success in bringing LVT within their armoury of tax-gathering measures to supplement local and national revenues. But why has this been so?

The evidence points to a lack of political willpower in the face of opposition from various professional groups and landowners, each with their own taxation agendas. Modern economists have tended to rally against Georgist doctrines, although proposals under consideration by Parliament certainly did not embrace George's root-and-branch single-tax panacea. Rating valuers and surveyors have stressed the difficulties of site valuation (despite the findings of the Whitstable pilot surveys) and still hold to the long-established rating procedures for a tax on the occupation of combined hereditaments of both land and buildings.

In envisioning future land policies, it is important to learn from the past: to identify what went right in these endeavours over the past century and what went wrong. What were the aims and objectives of the instigators of these efforts, and how well were these aims and objectives ultimately achieved?

Aims and Objectives of LVT Proponents

- A more rational system of taxation for central and local purposes, which would aspire to the canons of Adam Smith: taxes based on the individual's ability to pay, certainty, convenience and economy.
- Extending taxation to encompass hitherto untaxed sources. Whereas in Britain property taxes for local government revenues are levied primarily on the occupier on the basis of beneficial occupation of a combined hereditament of land and buildings, proposals for LVT are directed to the ownership of land (whether occupied or not) and are assessed at site value.
- Adherence to the moral precept that land value increases not by any effort of its owners but because of the surrounding community, and that such increase in wealth should be returned to the community (in the form of tax revenue).
- Neutral and distributionally effective taxation. Taxes on economic rents from land, which is in inelastic supply, will not cause any change in demand or supply and cannot be shifted from the ownership of the land.
- Promotion and encouragement of investment in improvements to land rather than penalizing enterprise. The revenue from taxes on land would permit a reduction of taxes on buildings, which would encourage new construction.
- Encouraging land development. Taxing land at its value for highest and best use would penalize owners of undeveloped land.

What Went Right?

LVT proponents succeeded in focusing political attention on:

- Taxing land values, which otherwise would be likely to escape taxation measures.
- The moral aspects of fairer taxation—the idea that positive fiscal action was necessary to redistribute socially created wealth.
- Implementing economic and taxation principles (i.e., a tax on economic rent) that would minimise intrusion upon and distortion of the economy.

- Taxing the owners of land, who were the real beneficiaries of enhanced land values, rather than the land's occupiers.
- Taxing basic land values rather than penalising investment by taxing buildings and improvements to land.
- Bringing land into "production," using land more efficiently, and discouraging owners from delaying development of their land in anticipation of rising markets.
- Demonstrating that land taxation is a practical possibility: H.M. Wilks's land valuation exercises in Whitstable in 1963 and 1973 showed that neither the valuation process nor identification of ownerships constituted an intractable problem.
- Addressing taxation in the legislative drafting of successive parliamentary bills, culminating in the London Rating (Site Values) Bill prepared by the London County Council in 1938. (This may well form a precedent for any future legislation.)
- Solving previous technical difficulties with the "sanctity of contracts" in distributing the land tax burden. For example, the Valuation and Rating Act (Scotland) 1956 abolished owners' rates in Scotland and, in parallel, reduced rents in existing leases without any shattering legal, moral or practical consequences (Prest 1981, 143). Another example of a distributive solution follows the procedure for allocating Schedule A income tax assessments and as also referred to in the Simes Committee (1952) report and previously in the 1938 LCC Bill.

What Went Wrong?

- Most of the proposals were piecemeal and selective (see schedule of legislative proposals, Table 5) and were inspired more by individual or unilateral efforts rather than coordinated policies.
- There was no overall national strategy for universal application to all land values throughout the U.K. Most of the proposals submitted by local authorities were targeted for local expenditures in their own local area. Some of the private members' bills were drafted as adoptive measures for local authority pursuance, although others had national expenditure in their sights.
- There was no consensus on proposals' raison d'être. The two government proposals that were enacted, in 1910 and 1931, were originally drawn as national taxation measures for central resources, but under pressure from local authorities it seemed likely that if the acts had become operative, some part of the tax collected would have gone to local resources.

- Land value taxation continued to be perceived as too complex to be practical. This was the clear downfall of the 1910 act: four different kinds of values had to be ascertained, improvements had to be valued, and the taxes fell in an irregular and partial fashion.
- Bad timing. The 1931 act emerged in difficult economic and political circumstances and was abandoned by a succeeding government within a year of reaching the statute book.
- The government did not adequately stand up to opposition. Lobbying by landowners and their professional advisers confounded the operation of the government's own legislation and the enactment of any of the multitude of bills originating from private members and local authorities.
- The tax on land values was, in the main, regarded as an addition to or partial substitution for existing rates; there was no clear-cut transference of the rates burden to owners.
- The case for land taxation for revenue-raising purposes became entangled with the development charges under the 1947 Planning Act. The majority report of the Simes Committee of Enquiry (1952) cited this as its principal reason for recommending against pursuing the rating of site values per se. But, as enumerated in Chapter 7, the abolition of these development charges in 1953 subsequently invalidated this reasoning.

Summary

There have been many attempts over the years to introduce a form of LVT as an annual tax in Britain. Analysing the degrees of success and failure of past attempts provides a basis for formulating new proposals. But first we will shift our focus from LVT as an annual tax to other forms of LVT that capture the capital value of land for the benefit of the community, starting with recoupment via ownership.

■ **ANNEXE TWO**

Features of Main Legislative Attempts up to 1939 (World War II)

Information on the following measures was derived from evidence presented to the Simes Committee (1952).

Land Value Duties Act, 1910

In the early years of the twentieth century, many local authorities had interested themselves in the rating of site values, and the next legislative step was to enact the land value duties under the Finance Act, 1910, which comprised:

- an increment value duty on land sold or subject to long leases, payable on transfer or death of owner;
- a reversion duty of 10 percent on the termination of a lease of 21 years or over except on and with purely agricultural value;
- an annual levy of one half penny in the £ of capital value on undeveloped land other than house gardens, land with a purely agricultural value, or land worth not more than £50 an acre; and
- a 5 percent levy on mineral rights.

The legislation was extremely complicated. It should be noted, however, that there was no attempt to implement a general levy on the site value of land. Of more direct interest in our enquiries is the definition of site value, on which these duties were to be based. The assessable site value was defined as the sum that the property would realize if offered for sale by a willing seller in the open market. As such, it would be subject to ordinary rates and taxes and in its actual condition as regards buildings and other structures, subject of fixed charges, public rights of way and user, easements and restrictive covenants, less any value in respect of:

- buildings and any other structures, and all growing timber, fruit trees etc.;
- works or capital expenditure by the owner, executed or incurred for the purpose of improving the value of land as building land for any business or industry other than agriculture.

Before the act of 1910 had been passed, the government promised, after protests from local authorities, to allocate to them half the proceeds of these duties.

By the Revenue Act of 1911, however, this concession was suspended up to 31 March 1914, and the basis of distribution was never determined.

After a change in government in 1918, political pressure was brought to bear for an abolition of the 1910 act, and in 1922 it was finally repealed.

Finance Act, 1931

Taxation of land values for national purposes was, for the second time, provided for in the Finance Act, 1931. The Commissioners of Inland Revenue were directed to ascertain by 1 January 1932 the value of each land unit, which was defined as "the amount which the fee simple thereof with vacant possession might have been expected to realize upon a sale in the open market on the valuation date upon the assumptions that there were not upon or in the unit any buildings, elections, or works, except roads etc. or anything growing on the unit except grass etc."

But following a national economic and financial crisis and the formation of a coalition government, valuation under this 1931 act was suspended by the Finance Act of 1932, and its LVT provisions were finally repealed by the Finance Act of 1934.

Provisions of the LCC Bill: London Rating (Site Values) Bill, 1938–1939

The London County Council (LCC) resolved in 1938 that the current burden of local expenditure should be transferred wholly or partly to a rate on site value. Consequently, the LCC promoted a private bill to achieve these aims. Its main provisions were:

- A valuation was to be made of the annual site value of every land unit, this being defined as the annual rent that the land comprising the land unit might be expected to realise if demised with vacant possession at the valuation date in the open market by a willing lessor upon a perpetually renewable tenure upon the following assumptions, namely, that at the valuation date:

  a. there were not upon or in that land unit:
  - any buildings, erections or works except certain roads; and
  - anything growing except grass, heather, gorse, sedge or other natural growth;
  b. the annual rent had been computed without taking into account the value of any tillages or manures or any improvements for which any sum would by law or custom be payable to an outgoing tenant of a holding;
  c. the land unit were free from any encumbrances except such of the following encumbrances as would be binding on a purchaser:

easements; rights of common; customary rights; public rights; liability to repair highways by reason of tenure; liability to repair the chancel of any Church; liability in respect of the repair or maintenance of embankments or sea or river walls; liability to pay any drainage rate under any statute; restrictions upon user which have become operative imposed by or in pursuance of any Act or by any agreement not being a lease.

- The incidence of the rate was to be upon the respective owners of the site value (generally by means of deduction from rent), any past or future provision in contracts, having the effect of relieving in whole or in part any person entitled to receipt of rent from any liability, to be void in respect of the site value rate. The occupier, in normal cases, would pay the rate in the first instance.
- The amount of the annual rate on site values, as from April 1941, was to be two shillings in the £ (10 percent), and it was to be collected by the rating authority with the general rate, although there would have been a separate demand note for the site rate.

Subsequently, the Speaker of the House of Commons ruled in 1939 that, because of the importance of issues raised, the LCC bill ought to be introduced as a public bill. But this proposal was later refused by the House, and the bill failed to pass.

CHAPTER SIX

Recoupment via Ownership

In this chapter we consider LVT as an available choice of capital exactions in line with government policies for land use and development. We first consider the policy of recoupment of development value via ownership, sometimes known as land banking, which is not, strictly speaking, the same as levying taxes, but is a means of land value capture for the benefit of the community. Although not previously unknown, this process gained impetus in the immediate post–World War II years. Hence, we treat it as an historical precursor to the other, later attempts at value capture.

In the planning and development of towns and regions, public-sector acquisition has a far-ranging role in advancing a government's social, economic and political objectives. Governments can recoup development land value by forward purchase of real estate on the part of an acquiring authority, ensuring value capture to the community by positive and advance action. To view this process in its wider scope we first examine examples in overseas countries, and then we compare and contrast those efforts with past and present U.K. procedures.

Overseas Practices

United States

Large-scale land acquisition (and subsequent disposal) was instrumental in opening up the United States during its westward development, with a view to passing the land on to the private sector. As Strong (1979, 26) describes, after the creation of the U.S., all new acquisition of land was carried out by the federal government. The new land, outside of Texas and Hawaii, became part of the national public domain. All told, between 1803 and 1867, 1.8 billion acres, or 79 percent of the present area of the U.S., passed into the public domain. The average cost of the bought land was four cents per acre. The U.S. government's prevailing policy, at least for the first 100 years of the public domain, was that it was desirable and urgent for the nation to expand its land holdings and that the land should be committed to private ownership.

Strong also points out:

> The government's disposal policy was shaped by several factors, whose relative weights varied over time. These factors were: the desire to get land settled and into productivity as rapidly as possible, the need for revenue for the federal treasury, the need for dispersed settlement of the West to provide a place for immigrants and to increase safety from the Indians, the commitment to reward soldiers with land, and the aim of promoting self-sufficiency in the newly formed states. (1977, 27–31)

A prime example of U.S. governmental disposal policy, in an endeavour to "open up" the country and make the West more accessible to settlers, is the gifting of land to railroad companies. Between 1850 and 1900 some 91 million acres were so given by federal grant and another 49 million acres were donated by the states. But the government's hope to profit from rising land values in adjacent retained land proved illusory, and it did not even recover the value of the land given to the railroads. Nevertheless, the rapid settlement of the country, and its consequent effects on the nation's development and prosperity, can be claimed as the most important returns to the government on the railroad-land investment.

Although government policy up to the close of the nineteenth century dictated that public-domain land should be returned to private hands as rapidly as possible, Strong (1979, 34) explains that the twentieth century saw a reversal of public policy. An increasing recognition of the finiteness of land resources and of the interconnections between land uses led to increasing support for public ownership and public control of land use. With a growing understanding that, while vast, U.S. land, water and mineral resources are not limitless, and that some of these resources have been squandered and others soon will be exhausted, a conservation ethic has taken root and is spreading.

The U.S. has begun to use public acquisition to deal with the inadequacies of past practices in private development. According to Roberts:

> Only recently—and invariably because of widespread urbanization and ecological concerns—have these inherited notions of property rights experienced erosion. This change has manifested itself in . . . the concept of private ownership of land shifting to account for the inadequacies of past practices to deal with the abuses of private development. The list of insults is long and shameful and the consequence has been that conservation concerns have succeeded to a new position in the priority of considerations regarding the use of land. (1977, 202)

In line with these aspirations for public acquisition, Kehoe (1976, 3) argues that community ownership of land would result in a radical alteration of the basis of current urban social and economic order. He points out that land ownership has been and still is the mainstay of individual wealth, social worth and political influence in a community. Taking this argument still further, Penalosa contends in Kehoe (1976, 9) that there is still another consequence of the private ownership of land: the systematic impoverishment of the poor. However, the other side of the argument is that it is the impossibility of acquiring an interest in land that still prevents ordinary individuals in many undeveloped countries from accumulating even modest levels of capital wealth.

France

Public-sector acquisition has been valuable in strengthening land-use controls in France. Strong (1979, 142) particularly describes the designation of large areas as zones in which acquisition could occur, with restrictions on the actual purchase of lands more critical for development, farming or resource protection. These approaches result in a rough sort of equity that dampens the grosser excesses of speculation while leaving the bulk of land transaction in private hands. Currently France is attempting to affect the use of all land in urban areas by enacting zoning-type regulations, but there have been some doubts about the efficacy of this procedure. As a coordinating measure, both large-scale development and the preservation of open land have relied on the land-banking process to control the future use of the land, which for the most part has been positive.

On a key example of large-scale land banking in the Marseilles area, Strong further comments:

> One can say that the land question acquisition program moved rapidly and smoothly, evidencing considerable cooperation among the state, local government, and the private sector. Buying large tracts in advance of public awareness of development plans established market value; this, combined with the existence of the eminent domain power, made it possible to buy the land at reasonable prices. State initiatives in providing the bulk of the funds for land acquisition, in authorizing direct state acquisition, with its state-local-private sector management, have been critical. So, too, has been the leadership exerted by the Marseilles Chamber of Commerce and Industry. (1979, 209)

The Netherlands

Public acquisition was essential in the Netherlands for providing the infrastructure needed for housing in the low-lying land reclaimed from the sea. It also became significant for controlling land price on disposal. For decades most Dutch municipalities customarily have bought land a few years in advance of development, prepared it for development, and then sold or leased the actual development sites, retaining a substantial portion of the land for roads, parks and community facilities.

In the Netherlands, the long experience of municipal land acquisition of the urban-extension type has so affected expectations that speculation in development land is considerably restricted. The Dutch land-acquisition procedure is based on the Expropriation Act, which gives municipalities the power to expropriate land located in an area of an approved extension plan on the basis of existing market prices for current land use (Lichfield and Darin-Drabkin 1980, 200). This basis means that land need not be acquired far in advance of need, since the acquisition is in accord with current use, thus holding down carrying costs.

Strong (1979, 100) also confirms that, as part of this process, land banking has been used as a first step towards plan implementation, making it possible to provide housing sites at moderate cost and to develop land in an efficient and orderly manner. Intentions to garner increases in land value for municipalities have not always been effectively realised. In any event, landowners recognise that little, if any, opportunity for speculation exists, and because they generally believe that municipalities pay a fair price for land, they acquiesce to municipal proposals.

Sweden

In Sweden land banking has historically been the principal tool for implementing urban development for medium and large Swedish cities. Strong cites the following prime example:

> The city of Stockholm alone has acquired 138,000 acres since 1904, at a price of approximately $110 million. Its holdings outside of the city are twice as large as the area of the city itself. Most development in the region occurs on land held by the public for several decades and bought at or near farm value. (1979, 43)

British Practice

As a background to the history of the British system of recoupment via purchase, it is illustrative to quote the findings of the Uthwatt Committee on the subject:

> It should be observed that, although the system of recoupment enables a public authority to recover the whole or part of the increased value given to neighbouring lands by the execution of public works (as is the case under existing statutes), it is not strictly an application of betterment. The principle of betterment is that the public authority are entitled to require the owner of land increased in value by their works to pay over in money part of the increase which he hereby enjoys. In the case of recoupment, however the authority buy outright the land likely to be enhanced in value by their proposed works, paying the owner its current market value, and any profit they are able to make by developing or selling it is entirely theirs; there is, therefore, no need to ascertain how much of the profit is attributable to increase in value due to particular works and how much to other causes, and the major difficulty of the existing betterment system is avoided. (1942, 116–117)

Bearing this in mind, we now examine further the various forms of recoupment via ownership appearing over the years in Britain.

Pre–World War II Compulsory Acquisition

Historically, the clearest example of justification for compulsory acquisition is the royal prerogative to take land for the defence of the realm in times of emergency, while compensating the land's owners in full. Another example is the "inclosures" of land mandated by private local acts of Parliament in the eighteenth and nineteenth centuries; these procedures were eventually formalised under the Inclosure Act of 1845. Of the more than 4,000 inclosure acts that were passed in the eighteenth and nineteenth centuries,[1] the great majority were private acts. The objective of the earliest legislation was to facilitate the inclosure of common land, but by 1876 perceptions had changed: the Commons Act of that year emphasised the regulation of commons rather than inclosure, and the inclosure movement slowed. In 1913 a select committee of the House of Commons concluded that "regulation of commons as distinguished from inclosure would be everywhere beneficial to all the interests concerned" (DEFRA 2000, iv), and the last application for inclosure under the inclosure acts was made in 1914.

In the formative era of the nineteenth century, the majority of compulsory-acquisition activities were carried out by private companies; this process endured for more than 50 years. Thus, at the beginning of the Industrial Revolution, the use of compulsory powers was tailored to serve private interests, albeit to supplement public-interest goals. A prime example of this process was when the construction and growth of the early railways necessitated the application of compulsory powers, as Millichap explains:

> The expansion of the railways in the early part of the nineteenth century first prompted the substantial growth in the application of powers of compulsory acquisition. With their need for relatively straight tracks and wide curves, railways were particularly susceptible to economic extortion by owners of land along proposed routes, and powers of compulsory acquisition soon became essential to economic development as a corollary both to their peculiar needs and to the obligations to the public which they were forced by Parliament to assume. Similar considerations apply equally to gas, electricity, water and sewerage undertakings; all require powers of compulsion, for all involve both the acquisition of land for exclusive use for the erection of main installations, and the acquisition of lesser interests, such as rights over other people's land, for the laying of pipes and cables. (1999, 1–2)

---

1. See also *Rural Rides*, collection of essays by William Cobbett, published in 1830, which originally appeared in the *Political Register*, recording actual observation of rural conditions (standard ed., 3 vols., by G.D.H. and M. Cole, 1930).

To enable local authorities to buy the land they needed for public works without having to pay extortionate prices, Parliament enacted the first Lands Clauses Consolidation Act in 1845, which achieved a more unified acquisition process and a unified code of compensation. This was followed by the Acquisition of Land (Assessment Compensation) Act (1919) and the Acquisition of Land (Authorisation Procedure) Act (1946), which eventually ensured standard procedures of compulsory acquisition of almost universal application. This act originally applied mainly to acquisition by local authorities, but later acts have substantially widened its scope to include acquisition by government departments.

Post–World War II Compulsory Acquisition

Since World War II, Britain has captured a great deal of the increases in land values through public acquisition of land for development or redevelopment and subsequent renting or leasing. In this way, increases in land values flow to the public purse.

In Britain public authorities are given wide-ranging powers to buy land for any "planning purpose"; this departs from other countries' restrictions on land use for "public purposes" (Heap 1996, 321–322). In this chapter we focus on those occasions where public purchase has been employed to recoup rises in land value through public development to the community (on a leasehold or freehold basis). This includes the redevelopment of bomb-damaged and obsolete areas after the war (TCPA1944, TCPA1947); the building of some 30 new towns, starting in 1946 (NTA1946); the expansion of existing towns (TDA1952); and the redevelopment and regeneration of obsolete areas by government-appointed urban development corporations (LGPLA1980).

Town and Country Planning Act, 1944 (TCPA1944). Heap (1996, 321–322) explains that, despite its title, the major portion of TCPA1944 dealt not with planning but with land acquisition and new powers of acquiring land compulsorily (and, in exceptional cases, very speedily) for a variety of purposes, in areas of extensive war damage ("blitzed" areas) and areas of bad layout and obsolete development ("blighted" areas). This act introduced the important new concept of positive town planning, by empowering local planning authorities to undertake themselves the actual development of their own areas. It also introduced the "1939 standard" for compensation levels payable on the compulsory acquisition of land, a standard later abolished by the Town and Country Planning Act, 1947 (TCPA1947), and replaced by the principle of compensation based on the value for its existing use only.

New Towns Act, 1946 (NTA1946). NTA1946 provided for the creation of new towns by government-approved development corporations. Since 1946 some 30 new towns, each with its own corporation, have been established in Britain after land was designated for their sites by the government. The corporations were empowered to acquire, by agreement or compulsorily, any land within the designated area, any adjacent land that was required for the development of the town, or any other land required for the provisions of the town (Lichfield 1956, 243–244). The compensation code governing these transactions was identical to that governing any local authorities carrying out redevelopment under the Town and Country Planning Acts of 1944 and 1947. Corporations were also empowered to dispose of land, generally at market value, that they considered expedient for securing the development of the town.

Thus, the new-town corporations had the ability to capture development value for the benefit of the community, having acquired land under the earlier provisions, mainly under TCPA1947, based on existing use. But later the Town and Country Planning Act, 1959, and the Land Compensation Act, 1961 (LCA1961), provided that compensation would be the market value of the land, subject to the modification that the acquiring authority would not pay any increase or decrease in the value of the acquired land if the increase or decrease had been brought about by the scheme of development that gave rise to the need for compulsory purchase (Heap 1996, 330).

Town Development Act, 1952 (TDA1952). TDA1952 was passed in order to facilitate pre-existing arrangements with the new towns for housing overspill population and to provide an additional method whereby "large cities wishing to provide for their surplus population shall do so by orderly and friendly arrangements with the neighbouring authorities" (Lichfield 1956, 226). For land that was acquired in an approved town-development scheme, the operating authority had the powers of compulsory purchase under the 1944, 1947 and 1961 acts referred to above, as well as rights of disposal, appropriation and development.

Although town-development schemes governed by TDA1952 were introduced and processed in different formats and with differing participants than those of the new towns, the prospects for development value capture by the operating authority were similar, and both processes are prime examples of recoupment via ownership.

Comprehensive Development: Town and Country Planning Act, 1947 (TCPA1947). Under TCPA1947, a local planning authority could initiate the development of any area by defining it as an area of comprehensive development (CDA) in the development plan. A CDA was defined as an area that should be developed or redeveloped as a whole for the purpose of dealing satisfactorily with extensive war damage or conditions of bad layout or obsolete development; for relocating population or industry or replacing open space in the course of the development or redevelopment of any other area; or for any other purpose specified in the plan (Lichfield 1956, 203). Once a comprehensive development area had been designated and approved by the government minister responsible, the local authority could purchase the land, by agreement or by taking compulsory powers of acquisition. Compensation under TCPA1947 would have been based on existing use or, later, under LCA1961, at market value, disregarding the effects of the scheme on that value.

Under this arrangement, local authorities disposing of land had the opportunity to capture development value. Many of the important CDAs involved redevelopment on major town centres; in these cases, local authorities were encouraged to enter into partnership schemes with commercial development companies. These partnerships generally involved granting a ground lease to the developer (usually for 99 years, but sometimes for even 125 years) under the condition that the developer would fund and build an agreed scheme.

In the early partnerships, local authorities concentrated on achieving ground rents to cover their outlay costs, including their borrowing charges. But gradually, as local authorities gained experience and expertise, the formulae for the calculation of appropriate ground rents became more sophisticated and evened up the financial expectations of the respective parties. It then became usual that the developer would receive a required minimum return on approved outlay, and the local authority would obtain a guaranteed minimum ground rent based on a residual deduction from an agreed estimate of the developer's eventual rentals for the completed scheme. However, if that estimate of rentals was to be exceeded, upon completion the excess would usually be shared; this would then be built into the ground rent payable to the local authority. Initially, it was normal to fix such a ground rent for long periods without review, but over the years, as awareness of the prospects of rising values grew, it became standard practice to introduce more frequent rent reviews into the ground lease, thus securing to the local authority an increasing share of value capture.

Local Government, Planning and Land Act, 1980 (LGPLA1980). LGPLA1980 broke new ground in the sphere of land development and planning control by empowering the Secretary of State to designate an area of land, usually derelict and run-down (often the inner core of an old town), as an "urban development area" and to establish an urban development corporation to regenerate the area (Heap 1996, 460).

These corporations were given powers to acquire, reclaim and dispose of land and other property and to carry out building and other operations for the benefit of the schemes undertaken. They could acquire land by agreement or compulsorily by vesting under the compensation provisions of LCA1961, which specifically excluded any increase in the value of the acquired land brought about by the scheme itself, so the corporations had opportunities for development value capture that were similar to those afforded new towns and town-development operations. A number of corporations were founded in various towns, each with its own special act. The case of London Docklands illustrates this process.

The London Docklands Development Corporation (LDDC) was established on 2 July 1981, under the provisions of s. 136 of LGPLA1980, in response to the severe economic, physical and social damage caused to East London by the closure of London's docks. As described in LDDC (1998, 1), the London Docklands Urban Development Area (UDA) covered eight and a half square miles (2,146 ha.), extending six miles (10.8 km) down river from London Bridge to the south and Tower Bridge to the north, and comprised parts of the London boroughs of Southwark, Newham and Tower Hamlets.

The LDDC's strategy has been to correct market failures and to create the circumstances and, in particular, transportation infrastructure in which private investment would fund the economic regeneration of London Docklands, while improving the social infrastructure and public amenities from their low base.

Since 1981, as a result of the LDDC's endeavours, the population of London Docklands has increased from 39,400 to more than 80,000, and the number of jobs has risen from 27,200 to 72,000. Some 21,600 new dwellings have been built and 2.3 million square meters of new commercial buildings have been completed, spurring an increase in the number of businesses from 1,000 to 2,450. Public investment of £1.799 billion has generated £6.5 billion of private investment. However, the regeneration of Docklands is far from complete; despite the massive improvement so far, it will take decades to realise the full potential of the area and to eliminate all of the dereliction and decay.

Considered as an act of positive regeneration combined with development value capture, London Docklands is an outstanding example of what can be achieved by the process of recoupment via ownership. But the process is ongoing, and the story is not complete. From the government's viewpoint, the greatest and the most worthwhile return on its investment in the project is the overall economic regeneration of London Docklands.

Key Features

To summarise the main process of recoupment via ownership in post–World War II Britain, which Grant has described as "pre-empting the accrual of value," we can do no better than to quote his succinct exposition of some of the key features:

The legislative scheme for new towns exempted the development corporations from having to pay enhanced land values when acquiring land in their designated areas. In calculating compensation, the valuer was entitled to assume that planning permission would be granted for the development for which the land was being acquired (e.g., housing, commercial, industrial), but to do so in a "no-scheme world," ignoring the whole of the new-town development that was taking place, and hence the services that the scheme was bringing to the area. This had the effect of enabling the corporations to acquire land net of betterment, yet being able in due course to sell land on at market value. A similar formula was extended in due course to the town expansion schemes [under the Town Development Act 1952]. It was later applied also to urban development corporations, but its application within existing urban areas was to prove more difficult than for Greenfield sites. Projects to provide infrastructure some time after the designation of the area also confronted the problem that investment expectations had already risen (which indeed was one of the objectives of the exercise), yet the land that was needed for, say, a new road scheme, could be acquired only at the lower statutory value. (Grant 1999, 62)

Other Forms of Recoupment

Britain has also captured value from the nationalisation of natural resources such as coal (CIA1949, OCA1958), oil/gas (GPPA1944, CSA1964), both offshore (OGEA1982) and on-shore, and the spectrum of radio waves. Nationalisation of underground deposits of coal, with compensation paid to the owners, was initiated in the Coal Act of 1930. This enabled the National Coal Board to grant licenses for the use of the nationalised rights subject to obtaining a planning permission. The same system applies to open cast mining, which began during World War II, but no compensation was paid to the landowners, although restoration of the surface was the responsibility of the promoters.

For oil/gas, the government assumed ownership of both on-shore and off-shore deposits. It was thus able to grant licenses to explore and, when appropriate, to operate, and to garner income in the form of royalties from the drilling operators.

These principles were also applied to licenses for the use of the spectrum of radio waves. The income was secured as a result of open auction bidding by intending licensees to run the next generation of mobile phones. In April 2000 the auction for the next third-generation (3G) mobile phone licenses in the U.K. resulted in a £22.47 billion (US$35.4 billion) windfall to the British government, and an even higher figure of £30.4 billion (US$46.1 billion) was subsequently achieved by the German government for its grant of similar licenses (as reported by BBC Business News).

However, this over-propitious start may well have heralded some unforeseen consequences: BBC Business News (2000, 1) also reported that after the early end of Italy's auction of third-generation mobile phone licenses, the Italian government was left with the unwelcome prospect of pocketing far less from the sale than it had hoped. Overall, the story of 3G license auctions across Europe has been one of unpredictable results and widely varying fortunes: the U.K. and German governments both raised billions of dollars more than they had anticipated, but an auction in the Netherlands fell flat, generating little more than one-quarter of what the government had hoped.

Future Prospects

Difficulties currently exist in Britain in applying public acquisition towards securing development land capture; compulsory acquisition as a purchasing process has fallen out of favour for a number of reasons. In Chapter 11 we consider future prospects of recoupment via ownership, in the light of prospective changes to the compulsory-acquisition process recently anticipated by the British government.

Summary

We have looked at the various ways governments can recoup value (usually termed *development value*) by ensuring early ownership of land or of any other national asset capable of accruing such future value. We now identify and consider other LVT measures directed toward capturing capital value for the benefit of the community.

CHAPTER SEVEN

Recouping Betterment via the Town and Country Planning System

T his chapter, contributed by Nathaniel Lichfield, is based on Lichfield and Connellan's working paper *Land Value Taxation in Britain for the Benefit of the Community: History, Achievements and Prospects* (1998; see also Appendix A for further reference).

Introduction

In this chapter on capturing value for the community by recouping betterment, we define *betterment* as the increase in land value arising from development activity. The objective of betterment legislation is to capture this development value for the benefit of the community, as confirmed by the Uthwatt Committee that "The principle of betterment [legislation] is that the public authority are entitled to require the owner of land increased in value by their works to pay over in money part of the increase which he hereby enjoys" (1942, 116).

History of Betterment Legislation

Betterment has been collected in Britain under ad hoc legislation for many centuries. In 1909 it was incorporated into the town and country planning system; since then it has gone through many changes, particularly after World War II.

Two threads in the fabric of Britain's history indicate the application of the principle of betterment in legislation:

- payment *according to* benefits received or dangers avoided, most frequently represented by sewers and drainage rates; and
- payment (whether by direct charge or set off against compensation) *in respect of* benefits received by public improvements, e.g., through the widening of roads.

The first thread remains unbroken from the Middle Ages; nowadays it makes an appearance in the differential rates under the Land Drainage Act, 1930. The second thread first appeared in 1662 but disappeared after a few years and did not reappear until about 1830. Thereafter, although somewhat tenuous for long periods, this thread persisted, and it appeared in full strength and colour in the London County Council Improvement Acts of the 1890s and in the Town Planning Acts from 1909 onwards.

Evolution of the British Planning System, 1909–1991

The planning of towns is an ancient art and science, but it is mainly in the twentieth century that governments around the world intervened to ensure its application in their country. Britain did so in 1909, instituting a statutory planning system consisting of statutes, regulations and guidance. It is within this system that the statutory planning process is carried out.

Pre–World War II

Town and country planning as a governmental task developed from public-health and housing policies (Ashworth 1954, chap. 1). The nineteenth century's increases in population and the subsequent growth of towns due to immigration from rural areas led to public-health problems that demanded a new role for government. The first statute, the Housing, Town Planning, Etc., Act of 1909, empowered local authorities to prepare town planning schemes with the general object of "securing proper sanitary conditions, amenity and convenience," but only for land that was being developed or appeared likely to be developed (Cullingworth and Nadin 1994, 2–4). After World War I, this legislation was revised to form the Housing and Town Planning Act of 1919. The preparation of schemes was made obligatory on all borough and urban districts having a population of 20,000 or more. Although some procedural difficulties were removed, no change was made in the basic concepts.

As difficulties increased, further legislation was passed. The Town and Country Planning Act of 1932 (TCPA1932) aimed to control the development of both urban and rural land so as to secure proper sanitary conditions, amenity and convenience; to preserve existing buildings, other objects of architectural, historic or artistic interest, and places of natural interest or beauty; and generally to protect existing amenities (Jennings 1946, 12). It extended planning powers to almost any type of land, whether built up or undeveloped. TCPA1932 schemes relied on *zoning* as their main tool; land was zoned for particular uses, with provision for such controls as limiting the number of buildings and the space around them.

But Britain's planning system between the first and second world wars was defective in several ways: it was optional for local authorities; planning was local in character; central government had no effective powers of initiative or of coordinating local plans; and the issue of compensation deterred local authorities from applying effective measures (Cullingworth and Nadin 1994, 9).

Changes During World War II

TCPA1932 was amended by the Town and Country Planning Interim Development Act of 1943. This related only to the interim development period (the period between when a resolution to prepare a scheme takes effect and the date on which the scheme becomes operative). It introduced two changes: it brought the whole of England and Wales under planning control; and interim development decisions became enforceable in the interim period (Jennings 1946, 7).

Post–World War II

The new Labour government, after the end of World War II, introduced the Town and Country Planning Act of 1947 (TCPA1947). It differed from TCPA1932 in that it introduced "development plans" instead of planning schemes. Whereas previously the rules for granting permission for development were stated in the planning scheme, which was a "local law" for the area, under TCPA1947, development (to works on or under land or a material change of use) could take place only with a specific permit (Lichfield and Darin-Drabkin 1980, 137). TCPA1947 provided the whole country with powers of development control, which became mandatory and not permissive. Thus, it brought all development under control, with only minor exceptions, by making it subject to planning permission.

The Town and Country Planning Act of 1968 (TCPA1968) also brought about a major shift in planning philosophy, in the scope and content of plans. Whereas TCPA1947 was mainly concerned with land use, TCPA1968 emphasised major economic and social forces, as well as broad policies and strategies for large areas (Cullingworth and Nadin 1994, 52). TCPA1968 also ushered in an era of centralised policy making that continued into the 1990s (Cullingworth and Nadin 1994, 53). TCPA1968 was later repealed and consolidated with the Town and Country Planning Act, 1971.

Current Position

The Town and Country Planning Act of 1990 also consolidated earlier legislation; it was soon modified by the Planning and Compensation Act of 1991 (PCA1991), which retained the major principles of the acts of 1947 through 1971 but brought changes to the planning framework, for example, as related to development control.

Section 54A of PCA1991 introduced what has come to be called the plan-led system:

> Where, in making any determination under the planning Acts, regard is to be had to the development plan, the determination shall be made in accordance with the plan unless material considerations indicate otherwise.

But this meant that the development rights for any parcel of land, and thereby the consequential land value, could not be determined with any certainty in advance of the decision on the planning application, and, should there be an appeal to the Minister or the courts, the decision would flow from them. Although the balance shifted in PCA1991, the same uncertainty still remained. In Chapter 14 and Appendix D, we examine the government's latest proposals to update the British planning system and consider their likely effects upon this issue.

Compensation and Betterment in Principle

Just as the concept of betterment emerges when development values rise, so does compensation to owners when their land loses development value. Betterment and compensation—the inseparable twins of the financial provisions of planning legislation—are better known in the United States as "windfalls" and "wipe-outs" (Hagman and Misczynski 1978, chaps. 1, 17). This principle was recognised in the 1909 Housing, Town Planning, Etc., Act and continued in the Town and Country Planning Act, 1932 (Uthwatt, paras. 231, 271–274).

In 1942 Lord Reith, the Minister of Works, appointed experts to examine the subject of compensation-betterment and reconstruction after World War II. These experts formed the Expert Committee on Compensation and Betterment (Uthwatt Committee), 1942, which fully introduced the link between compensation and betterment:

> In this connection two well recognized facts must be borne in mind. The first is that potential development value created by the expectation of future development is spread over many more acres than are actually required for development in the near future or are ever likely to be developed. The second is that wisely imposed planning control does not diminish the total sum of land values, but merely redistributes them, by increasing the value of some land and decreasing the value of other land. (paras. 22–28)

It was these considerations that led the Uthwatt Committee to adopt the proposal initially put forward by the Barlow Commission (1940) for the unification of state landownership of development rights in undeveloped land; this was termed the "Development Rights Scheme" (para. 48). For developed land they recommended wider and simpler powers of purchase (sec. 50).

Compensation and Betterment in Practice

Town and Country Planning Act of 1947

Based on the general principles of the Uthwatt Report, the postwar Labour government enacted the Town and Country Planning Act of 1947 (TCPA1947), which nationalised development rights. With minor exceptions, no development would be allowed without the permission of the local planning authority. If permission were refused, no compensation would be paid, except in a limited range of special cases. If permission were granted, any resulting increase in land value would be subject to a development charge. The landowner had the right to continue the existing use of land so that any interference by the state would attract compensation (McAuslan 1984, 84; Cullingworth and Nadin 1994, 107).

Under TCPA1947, loss of development value due to the nationalisation of development rights (which was calculated to be the difference between the unrestricted use value and the existing use value) attracted compensation. This was based on admitted claims to an ex gratia fund of £300 million, plus one-seventh of the total fund for the accrued interest on the amount of the claim. The ex gratia fund was not described as "compensating" since, the government argued, none of the claims were payable under common law. A Central Land Board was also set up with powers to facilitate the supply of land at existing use prices.

But TCPA1947 did not work as expected. Land was being widely offered and bought at prices including the full development value, even though developers were to pay a development charge amounting to 100 percent of the land-value increase that resulted from development (Cullingworth and Nadin 1994, 10). This was largely due to the severe restrictions imposed on construction; building licenses were very scarce, and developers able to obtain them were willing to pay a high price for land upon which to build (Cullingworth and Nadin 1994, 108). Thus, developers often found themselves forced to pay more for land than its existing use value, which was all they should have been ready to pay (McAuslan 1984, 78).

Unscrambling: The Acts of 1953, 1954 and 1959

The new Conservative government in 1951 sought to remedy the problems of TCPA1947 through a series of measures under the Town and Country Planning Acts of 1953 and 1954. One of these measures was the abolition of the development charge and the termination of the Central Land Board. Abolishing the development charge caused land speculation: as long as owners could expect to receive only existing use value, there was little point in buying land to hold in anticipation of a price rise, but when development values were given back to private sellers, the prospect of speculative profits emerged again (Parker 1965, 67).

With the new scheme, the £300 million fund was extinguished as well. Instead of the compensation for development rights lost in 1947 being paid on a pro rata basis out of the fund, compensation was only payable when the loss was actually realised on refusal of permission. The local authority was made responsible to pay this compensation in cases where the claim attached to a site that was being compulsorily acquired. In other cases, it was the central government's responsibility (Parker 1965, 66).

The owners who sold their land privately in the market were now in a privileged position compared to owners whose land was subject to compulsory purchase (Parker 1965, 66). The former received the full market price for the property sold and retained the development value. The latter, however, only received existing use value because the development rights belonged to the state. This situation was tackled by the act of 1959, which re-established market price as the basis of compensation for compulsory acquisition (Parker 1965, 67). An owner could thus obtain the same price for his land irrespective of whether he sold it to a private individual or to a public authority, at least in theory. For the public authorities, land purchase suddenly became extremely costly (Cullingworth and Nadin 1994, 110).

Finance Act of 1965

A capital gains tax enacted in the U.K. by the Finance Act of 1965 allowed the taxation of capital gains made on the disposal of assets, including land, whether by outright sale or the grant of a lease. This tax has continued as an enduring feature of the British taxation system, except that it is now seen as part of general taxation and not specifically in relation to land itself. (In Chapter 12 we examine how this tax might be adapted more closely to the recoupment of betterment by capital levy.)

Land Commission Act of 1967

The Labour government of 1964 made another, quite different attempt to secure for the community a substantial part of the development value created by the community and to reduce the cost of land that authorities needed for essential purposes. A Land Commission was created to buy, by agreement or compulsorily, land suitable for development, with the objective of supplementing local authorities' powers to facilitate an orderly programme of approved development. The Land Commission was designed to be a site assembler; a planning agency to determine land use; and a development agency to manage, dispose of or develop land itself or engage either private or public developers. Thus, a central government agency was established to compete with the local authorities in determining where and how land should be used (McAuslan 1984, 78).

A betterment levy was introduced that was equal to a proportion of the development value on all land sold—either in the open market as a tax or in a sale to the Land Commission—and deducted against purchase at market value. Initially the rate of the levy was to be 40 percent to encourage early sale, and it was to increase over time (McAuslan 1984, 78).

Together with the betterment levy, the Labour government established a capital gains tax in the Finance Act of 1967. The tax was charged on the increases in the existing use value of land only, not on the increases in the development value, as in the betterment levy (Cullingworth and Nadin 1994, 111). Both of the taxes were measures for taxing the previously untaxed profits from land (Lichfield and Darin-Drabkin 1980, 144). But with a change of government, the Land Commission Act of 1967 was repealed in 1971 by the Conservatives (McAuslan 1984, 78).

Development Gains Tax

On 17 December 1973 the Conservative government's chancellor Anthony Barber announced a proposal to introduce legislation to alter the basis on which tax was charged on "substantial" capital gains arising on the disposal of land or buildings with development value or potential. He also announced that the legislation would provide for tax to be charged on the occasion on which a building (nonresidential) was first let, following "material development."

Soon after, however, there was a change of government. Following the general election of 28 February 1974, it fell to a new Labour chancellor to put these proposals into legislative clothing (Finance Act, 1974). The Labour government regarded this as an interim measure only, until a more far-reaching one could be found (Prest 1981, 96). Consequently, these limited arrangements for a development gains tax were replaced after 1 August 1976 by the more comprehensive Development Land Tax Act of 1976.

Community Land Scheme

The Labour government, elected in 1974, introduced its Community Land Scheme in two parts. The first was the 1975 Community Land Act, which provided wide powers for compulsory land acquisition, and the second was the Development Land Tax Act of 1976, which provided for the taxation of development values. This was going to be an achievement in "positive planning" (Lichfield and Darin-Drabkin 1980, 4) and in "returning development values to the community" (Cullingworth and Nadin 1994, 114).

The scheme, like its two predecessors, had little chance to prove itself. The economic climate of the first two years of its operation could hardly have been worse, and the consequent public-expenditure crisis resulted in a central control, which limited the scheme severely (Cullingworth and Nadin 1994, 114). With a change in administration, the Community Land Scheme was abolished by the Conservative Thatcher government in 1979. But the law as to the ownership of development rights remained the same, having survived the acts of 1953, 1954 and 1959. Development rights are still separated from the balance of the ownership title and are owned by the Crown, so that the denial of compensation for refusal of planning permission or imposition of unsatisfactory conditions still prevails.

Summary: Compensation and Betterment in 2004

The three postwar measures for betterment tax on development value in Britain, introduced by successive Labour administrations, were all withdrawn by the Conservative administrations that succeeded them. But one critically important feature of the 1947 act remains unaffected: the Crown continues to own all landed property development rights. Despite the amending planning legislation of subsequent governments and the Thatcher government's pressure for privatisation in the 1980s, these rights have not been returned to the property owners. Consequently, there is now no "compensation problem" to form the other side of the betterment coin: if a planning application is refused, or it is granted with conditions, no claim for loss of development rights can be admitted. Prest puts it succinctly: "[A]t least one thing does seem clear in the fog: the issue of planning compensation for planning refusal can be considered truly dead and buried" (1981, 189).

However, this now has an additional importance beyond the solution to the compensation problem when land value is mooted as a new taxation base. Any objections from landowners, for example, to an incremental betterment tax on the development rights, which they do not own but nevertheless can enjoy, as envisaged in the Uthwatt Report (1942, 135–154), would hardly make for a credible case at the Court of Equity.

Community Betterment from Development Value: An Evaluation of Past Proposals

We now evaluate the past proposals for community benefit from development value in order to draw lessons for the future.

What Went Right?

- After the Barlow Commission opened up the issue (RCDIP 1940), the Uthwatt Committee's classic report on compensation and betterment (Uthwatt 1942) provided a very good basis for postwar legislation and practice.

- Three successive Labour governments tried in quite diverse ways to tackle the issues of recoupment for the community. Through these attempts, vast experience was obtained of what could and could not be done.
- Despite opposition, developers have come to widely accept the thesis that some recoupment to the community is expected and accepted.
- It is now generally accepted that the community should not have to compensate landowners for restrictions on land value that result from denial of compensation for refusal or for composition of unsatisfactory conditions.

What Went Wrong?

- Betterment legislation became a political plaything. Each of the three Labour governments' ventures were opposed by the Conservatives and then unscrambled and/or repealed by them as soon as the opportunity arose and before the wrinkles could be ironed out. Furthermore, the Conservatives produced no reasonable replacement for the repealed systems, and, accordingly, there was no opportunity to amend any of the three ventures in the light of experience.
- All three Labour governments' attempts were very laborious and complex and therefore required a great deal of time to implement; none of them could be fully implemented before being repealed by the Conservatives.
- The Labour governments switched to a new concept each time around, missing opportunities to refine previously rejected schemes.
- The schemes themselves contained real defects, which have been recorded by commentators.

Flaws in the Labour Government Schemes

- The Town and Country Planning Act of 1947 (TCPA1947) failed because, while it allowed the private market to operate, the 100 percent development charge took away from the private market incentive to develop (Cox 1984, 82, in Blundell 1993, 5).
- Under TCPA1947, landowners retained land value increases that were not due to development or redevelopment. In practice, the majority of land value increases were of this kind, and therefore they could not be returned to the community (Blundell 1993, 12).
- TCPA1947 and the Land Commission Act of 1967 both encouraged speculation by leading landowners to believe that if their land increased in value they would not be liable to the development charge (Blundell 1993, 7–8).

- By 1952 the financial benefits of collecting development charges under TCPA1947 had proved discouraging:

  [T]he total sum received in development charges in the three and a half years which had elapsed since the "appointed day" was but £8.6 million, with a further £4.9 million set off against the compensation fund. The revenue which the charge was producing was negligible; the disincentive to development was massive. (Douglas 1976, 214)

- Similarly, under the Land Commission Act of 1967, the Commission completely failed to collect the forecast yield from levy; expecting to bring in £80 million in its first year, it in fact yielded a mere £15 million, and £32 million in the next year (1969–1970). And it had compulsorily purchased a derisory 2,207 acres of land and sold 913 acres (Cox 1984, 151).

- The Community Land Act of 1975 faced difficulties after the government's spending cuts in December 1976 reduced the borrowing capacity of local authorities by £70 million, and funding problems restricted their acquisition of land (Blundell 1993, 12). By April 1979 the Community Land Account was in deficit to the tune of £33 million (TCPA1997, 31, in Cox 1984, 187).

- The Community Land Act had many major problems. The government allowed no new staff to be hired; there were conflicts between planning, finance and surveying staff; lease provisions were for 99 years, but lending institutions preferred 125 years; some landowners were withholding deliberately; almost 98 percent of potential land was exempt because it was already held in land banks by statutory undertakers and builders; and there was a building slump, which meant that this exempted land was not used up as expected (TCPA1997, 31, in Cox 1984, 187–191).

In conclusion, the unscrambling resulted in the abandonment of compensation for injurious affection (i.e., depreciation) to land value, except for those whose claims for development values had been accepted by the Central Land Board as "unexpended balance of development value" in the TCPA1947 national valuation. These would have been met on refusal of planning permission, which would then capture that accepted claim value.

Even so, the present position is that planning compensation for betterment has now been abolished in these limited situations in which it was previously obtainable, by the Planning and Compensation Act 1991 (s. 31), except for relatively uncommon cases (Johnson et al. 2000, 245). But betterment in general, immediately post-TCPA1947, was effectively abandoned much earlier, with the abolition of the development charge and the termination of the Central Land Board in the acts of 1953 and 1954. We can say, however, that the spirit of betterment lived on in the later attempts to introduce betterment levy, development gains tax and development land tax. Although these particular measures also did not survive in securing betterment for the community, perhaps its long history will give it renewed strength for future reconsideration. With this in mind, in Chapter 12 we revisit this issue, with an examination of the possibility of reintroducing recoupment of betterment by capital levy.

Summary

Attempts by differing British governments to recoup betterment via the town and country planning system were largely frustrated. (Table 6 summarises the legislative underpinning for these attempts.) But, taking the wider view, betterment did indeed play a significant role in several value capture policies over the years.

TABLE 6: Summary of Post–World War II Betterment Legislation

Legislation	Provisions	Outcome
Town and Country Planning Act, 1947 (TCPA1947)	Inaugurated a Central Land Board to oversee the betterment and land assembly provisions of the act. Levied a development charge, based on enhancement of land value by grant of planning permission. Claims for loss of development value (due to nationalisation of those development rights) were invited, from a central fund of £300m.	Introduced by the post–World War II Labour government, TCPA1947 did not work as expected, and the disincentive to develop was very marked. The succeeding Conservative governments, in their Town and Country Planning Acts of 1953, 1954 and 1959, abolished development charges and the Central Land Board, and they ended the government obligation to distribute compensation to landowners.
Finance Act, 1965	Introduced a capital gains tax (CGT) payable upon the disposal of assets, including land, whether by outright sale or by the grant of a lease.	CGT continues as an enduring feature of the taxation system. It is now seen as part of general taxation and not specifically in relation to land itself.
Land Commission Act, 1967	Set up Land Commission to buy land for development and to act as a site assembler and development agency. Introduced a betterment levy, as a 40 percent proportion of development value on all land sold, either in the open market or to the Commission.	Introduced by a later Labour government, the Land Commission Act, 1967, failed to collect the forecast yield from the levy, and its land assembly results were disappointing. The succeeding Conservative government repealed the act and its measures in 1971.
Finance Act, 1974	Introduced a development gains tax on "substantial" capital gains arising upon the disposal of land or buildings with development value or potential, and on the first letting of a building following "material development."	First introduced as a proposal by Conservative government in Dec. 1973, this development gains tax was put into operation by the succeeding Labour government in 1974 as an interim measure only. It was eventually replaced by a development land tax in 1976.
Community Land Act, 1975	Provided wide powers of compulsory acquisition for the "Community Land Scheme," under which local authorities could purchase land for private-sector development and then dispose of that land by long lease.	Introduced by a Labour government but beset by national economic difficulties, this act failed in its aims, and the whole operation ran into deficit. Unsurprisingly, the Community Land Scheme was abolished by the succeeding Conservative government in 1979.
Development Land Tax, 1976	Taxed development gains, defined as the difference between market value and either current value or the cost of land plus special additions, whichever was higher. Tax was to be paid when land was developed or when land was sold or leased.	This was yet another frustrated attempt by a Labour government to tax betterment. When the Conservatives came to power in 1979, the tax was reduced to 60 percent, and it was eventually repealed completely in the Finance Act of 1985.

CHAPTER EIGHT

Contributions to Infrastructure Costs

T his chapter, contributed principally by Nathaniel Lichfield, is based on Lichfield and Connellan's working paper *Land Value and Community Betterment Taxation in Britain: Proposals for Legislation and Practice* (2000a) and continues our exploration of the ways different British governments tried to capture increases in land value for the community. Here we examine the recovery of contributions to infrastructure costs via the development process.

Background

There are other ways to tax land values besides annual imposts for governmental expenses, recoupment via purchase, or capital gains taxes upon acts of development. With the demise of the latest form of development land tax, another method of extracting value from the development industry for the benefit of the community has evolved: making developers fund contributions to infrastructure costs.

What Is Infrastructure?

At the risk of oversimplification, a town can be seen as comprising two main elements (Lichfield 1992, 1116): the terra firma, buildings and spaces that are the base for socio-economic activities (production, distribution, exchange and consumption, both by town residents and by those coming in from outside as regular commuters or irregular visitors); and the *infrastructure* of these activities, namely, "the underlying foundation or basic framework" (Longman 1984). Although there are many interpretations of underlying, there is general agreement that this includes transportation, telecommunication and their associated facilities (such as parking lots, bus and railway stations and telephone exchanges), as well as basic utilities (water, sewerage, waste disposal, gas and electricity).

Along with this physical infrastructure, others (see, for example, Loughlin 1985, 229–248) include the social infrastructure required to serve people, comprising all services that facilitate land development:

- services that make development *possible* (circulation streets, roads, water, sewerage, gas, electricity, telecommunications, street lighting, street cleaning and refuse services); and
- services that make development *acceptable* in terms of amenity (parks and amenity areas) and social overhead (schools, health and welfare services, libraries and other cultural facilities).

The "proprietary land unit" (Denman and Prodano 1972) defines what is on-site. Often private and public entrepreneurs provide the urban fabric in which the socio-economic activities are developed. The private or public landowner, developer or occupier in question would also provide, on-site, the relevant infrastructure for the development itself. Off-site, in the traditional division of labour in urban development, central and local government generally pays for physical and social infrastructure on behalf of taxpayers/ratepayers, together with ad hoc bodies on a commercial basis, for gas, electricity, water and sewerage. This division of investment is blurred at the edges. In a residential area, the developer will build the streets and gift them at the required standard to the local authority for maintenance; in a rural area, a local authority could build coastal protection works that are financed by taxing specific beneficiaries.

Thus, the building and running of a town is a mirror of our mixed economy. In this mix there is another ingredient: intervention by government (central and local combined) in the development, via the urban and regional planning system. Broadly, this has two aims: to remove impediments to the working of the market for both the private and public entrepreneurs and to regulate the market's activities in the "use and development of land in the public interest" (DoE 1983, para. 5). This combined intervention provides a wider definition of the infrastructure framework:

> all the supporting services required to ensure that land development takes place in a socially acceptable way; that is it does not intrude on the landscape, cause disturbance to neighbours, create traffic congestion, or overload the school system. This would seem to bring into this definition the avoidance of unfavourable externalities which arise from development. (Wakeford 1990, 2)

Current Funding of Infrastructure in Britain

Centuries of history are behind the funding of infrastructure in Britain; policies have evolved piecemeal with the growth in the infrastructure itself and with the multiplication of public agencies and powers related to the funding. For these reasons, current practice in British funding of infrastructure is complex (Lough-lin 1985). For our purposes here, we do not need a comprehensive description, but only a categorisation of different kinds of funding, as a context in which to consider "planning gain" later in the chapter. Following is a somewhat heroic attempt (Lichfield 1991).

Paid for by Central or Local Government and Recouped Out of Taxes, Business Rates and Council Tax

These are the traditional public works funded from public sources, such as roads, rail links, drainage, sewerage and parking lots. Generally, the funds are drawn in the form of taxes from the population as a whole, paid into one pool and distributed from the pool for specific works. For certain public works, particular funds may be earmarked or hypothecated, or there may be a special levy assessed on the beneficiaries of those works.

Paid for by a Statutory Undertaker with the Cost for a Specific Project Passed On to the Landowner/Developer

These are the traditional utility services, whether in public or private hands, or whether or not a monopoly. Their capital cost is typically met by developers as contributions, which are passed on to the consumers in the disposal price or to landowners in the reduced purchase price of land. An example is the levy for water and sewerage in the Water Act of 1989, supplementing the requisitioning required under the Water Act of 1945 by a system of general infrastructure charging, intended to fund capital costs incurred by undertakers when providing additional capacity.

Paid for by the Developer/Operator User Under the "Polluter Pays" or "User Pays" Principles

Public health. This involves construction that is regulated in the interests of public health, such as standards in sewers, water supply, etc., and access by streets to development that are initially constructed by the developer and then transferred to the local authority.

Environmental pollution. Emissions have been regulated in Britain since the Alkali Act of 1874, which has been the cornerstone of industrial air pollution control ever since. Modern concerns about environmental pollution (DETR 1994, part IV and Annex A) have added new dimensions. A more rationalised regulatory system was introduced in the Environmental Protection Act, 1990, with the adoption of the principle of "polluter or user pays" (both ex ante, in terms of tax, and ex post, in terms of damage caused) and the general move towards introducing financial incentives and disincentives.

In addition, since 1988, environmental assessment has been required as a preliminary to obtaining planning permission. Such assessments have been mandatory for projects where environmental pollution is fairly certain (e.g., power stations), and at the discretion of the local planning authority for projects where the environmental impacts are "likely to be significant" (e.g., from large-scale urban development) (DETR 1989c). In parallel legislation governing projects that fall outside the planning systems (e.g., forestry), the developer as potential polluter is called upon to pay an amount, by way of amelioration, proportional to the potential side effects (DETR 1989c).

Planning permission. When faced with an application for development, an authority may grant permission with or without conditions or refuse permission. Planning authorities have formidable powers of regulation over all physical development (new works and material change of use), with a complex array of typically insignificant exceptions. One objective of the Department of the Environment is to secure the "use and development of land in the public interest" (DETR 1997b, para. 5).

In general, the development control seeks to: improve the quality of development that is proposed, so affecting private development costs; minimise the divergence between private and social costs and benefits by ameliorating disbenefits in the proposals and thus internalising the costs; and coordinate with other development to minimise overall costs. Thus, development control can make the developer/landowner finance costs that would otherwise fall on the public purse.

The Shifting Frontier of Financing Infrastructure Development

Responsibility for the financing of the urban fabric for socio-economic activity and its infrastructure has been shifting in recent years towards developers in various ways. Utility services (water, gas, electricity, telecommunications, etc.) have been privatised. The public purse has been free to opt out of financing education and health services. The polluter pays or user pays principle makes operators and users, not the public purse, responsible for protecting the natural environment. Planning permission requirements transfer part of the cost and operation of developments from the public to the private purse. For matters that cannot be dealt with by planning conditions and that must be provided for under agreement, planning gain/obligation agreements transfer development cost to the developers. In cases where the cost of infrastructure being developed is too big to pass on to the landowner and/or developer as part of a planning permission, as in major road schemes, the financing has been sought entirely from the private sector, as provided for in the New Roads and Street Works Act of 1912.

In this the private sector seeks to recoup from sources that would otherwise be used by the public sector, such as tolls on the roads or recoupment from rising land values, on associated property. The Private Finance Initiative (PFI) has resulted in the private sector financing buildings for occupation by the public (RICS 1985, 5–7).

Shifts Through Ad Hoc Planning Agreements on Development Control

When local planning authorities decide to approve a planning application, they have been able to impose conditions on approval as they think fit (TCPA1971, sec. 29). But their freedom for imposing such conditions has been firmly constrained following court rulings against unreasonableness (DETR 1995). To overcome such constraints, local planning authorities have long been able to make deals with the developer that enable them to extend the scope of "conditions" (TCPA1932; TCPA1947). Although such agreements were originally conceived as a minor addition to planning control powers, their scope expanded considerably during the 1970s. The reasons were ones of expediency.

> The practice is a common-sense response to the contemporary situation. With the firm abandonment by the current government of the third post–World War II attempt at collecting betterment (in the Community Land and Development Land Tax Acts) landowners/developers/financial institutions can make fortunes out of a planning permit for using development rights which are still nationalised (the relevant provisions of the Town and Country Planning Act 1947 never having been repealed). Concurrently, under the present Administration, local government has restrictions on its financial resources and freedom to spend. Thus, the tax which planning gain imposes on the development industry, which it is generally prepared to accept to obtain the planning permission, offers a way of assisting local government in the financial trammels in which it finds itself, and comforts the taxpaying public in seeking social justice. (Lichfield 1989, 68)

These practices were recognised at the time by the government, which attempted to regularise them in a circular called *Planning Gain*:

> *Planning Gain* is a term that has come to be applied whenever, in connection with a grant or planning permission, a local planning authority seeks to impose on a developer an obligation to carry out works not included in the development for which permission has been sought, or to make some payment or confer some extraneous right or benefit in return for permitting development to take place.
>
> It is distinct from any alterations or modifications which the planning authority may properly seek to secure to the development that is the subject of the planning application [para. 2]. But the planning gain must be reasonable, depending on the circumstances [para. 5] and tests of such reasonableness are presented [paras. 6–8]. (DoE 1983)

The Conservative governments of the 1980s assumed direct and vigorous control over the expenditures of local authorities, whether from local taxation or government grant, which drove those authorities to seek ways to supplement their resources to meet their obligations. At the same time, landowners and developers were competing fiercely for permission to use the development opportunities on their land, which meant so much for them financially. During the boom of the economy and of the development industry during the 1970s, planning permission thus became a way that landowners and developers could accrue huge increases in the value of their land without having to pay for the development rights, beyond normal taxation. As a result, there arose without express legal sanction the system of planning gain, which amounted to the authority exacting contributions from the planning applicant, in money or in kind, towards the direct costs that would otherwise fall to the authority.

Under these pressures, the use of agreement grew. Recovery was made in practice not only to the 1932 and 1947 acts but also to three other legal bases: Section 52 of the Town and Country Planning Act of 1971, Section 111 of the Local Government Act of 1972, and Section 126 of the Housing Act of 1974. Besides these three, some additional powers were also obtained under local acts (McAuslan et al. 1984, 84).

In practice, only a small percentage of planning decisions in England involve planning agreements. The largest proportion of such agreements are concerned with regulatory matters (contracts, plans and drawings, building materials, etc.), and more than half of them deal with occupancy conditions (for example, restrictions required for sheltered housing, agricultural dwellings or social housing). Agreements also play an important role in funding the infrastructure necessitated by development (particularly roads) and in environmental improvement (such as landscaping). Only a very small number of agreements are concerned with wider planning objectives (Cullingworth and Nadin 1994, 115).

The Shortcomings of Planning Gain

Local authorities' experiences applying the national policy of planning gain in their locales have been very mixed. It has attracted many criticisms (Rosslyn Research 1990), and there is a considerable and rich body of literature on the topic (e.g., Healey et al. 1992). Following a review of some 12 agreements in action, Elson described the patchwork nature of the application of the policy in the following terms:

> A number of the schemes exceed the guidelines in Circular 22/83, by providing off site facilities mainly of use to the town or settlement, rather than exclusively for the development itself.... In some cases the facilities provided were not necessary to enable the development to proceed. In other cases, the facilities constituted requirements for a reasonable balance of uses, but their need was not

established in development plans.... Planning agreements are being used to commit different bodies to action (building roads, producing management plans or providing cash for long term maintenance). They appear to be important tools to commit the public sector to providing, or bringing forward, infrastructure.... In many cases agreements have an important role where sites are difficult to develop. We can see the presentation of a package of measures by developers which may involve some compromise in existing policies (e.g., green belt or densities).

In most of the cases here approvals and agreements have led, or significantly influenced, policies in development plans. In areas of high growth and development pressure local plans tend to be making sense of agreements across a range of sites, after most have been concluded, as well as others still under negotiation.... The schemes provide wide ranging off-site benefits. A number fall outside any definition of directly related infrastructure under the 1983 Circular, although others fall in a grey area between what might be regarded as strictly necessary for the scheme to proceed at all, and generally desirable local infrastructure or community provisions. . . . A wide variety of environmental, and some community, groups were involved in the negotiations surrounding agreements. These included Housing Associations, Parish Councils and local wildlife groups. . . . Many of the schemes suffered major time delays. A four year time span from application to approval, often including an appeal, was commonplace in the case studies. (1990, 35)

From Planning Gain to Planning Obligation

After some years of controversial practice, it became necessary for the Department of the Environment to attempt once more to clarify the situation. This it did initially in a consultation paper (DETR 1989a) that "substantially reaffirmed" the guidance in its circular 22/83 (DoE 1983), which the consultation paper was to supersede. In doing so, it introduced certain welcome clarifications, including the intention to replace the controversial term *planning gain* with the term *planning agreement*, because the name had "come to be used very loosely to apply to both normal and legitimate operations of the planning system and also attempts to extract from developers payments in cash or in kind for purposes that are not directly related to the development proposed but are sought as the price of planning permission. The Planning Acts do not envisage that planning powers should be used for such purposes, and in this sense attempts to exact 'planning gain' are outside the scope of the planning process" (DETR 1989a).

These clarifications were introduced by the Planning and Compensation Act of 1991 by substituting a new Section 106 in the Town and Country Planning Act of 1990, replacing Section 52 of the 1971 act. The policy change appeared in circular 16/91 (DETR 1991) as amended by circular 1/97 (DETR 1997a). Agreements have become obligations, which may be unilateral, not necessarily involving any agreement between a local authority and a developer at all

(Cullingworth and Nadin 1994, 115; Section 12 of the Planning and Compensation Act 1991, amending Section 106 of the Town and Country Planning Act 1990).

> Any person interested in land in the area of a local planning authority may, by agreement or otherwise, enter into an obligation (referred to . . . as a planning obligation) . . . restricting the development of the land in any specified way; requiring specified operations or activities to be carried out, in, on, under, or over the land; requiring the land to be used in any specified way; requiring a sum or sums to be paid to the authority on a specified date or dates or periodically. (Cullingworth and Nadin 1994, 115)

Although the new provisions adopted the term *planning obligations*, the term *planning gain* continues to be generally and loosely used. While introducing what has been called technical changes, planning obligations also reflected some of the fundamental criticisms of the former system. All in all, planning obligations have legitimised and institutionalised planning gain and clarified some important policy details, three of which stand out:

- planning obligations can be seen as part and parcel of the development application itself, even though the obligation relates to land other than that included in the initial application;
- the infrastructure that is the prime purpose of the obligation is no longer limited to the physical—it can also take in social facilities; and
- the gain can also directly relate to the conservation and/or preservation of the natural environment.

But while the switch from planning gain to planning obligation was a welcome clarification, and while it has affected procedural practice, it has hardly made any significant difference to everyday practice or to the acceptability of the system. Indeed, Elson's critique (1990, 35) is relevant to the critique of planning obligations.

Criticism was also levelled in the report of a working group of the Society for Advanced Legal Studies:

> The ability to create planning obligations is undoubtedly of benefit in connection with matters which cannot otherwise be dealt with. But their use is too often contentious. The Committee on Standards in Public Life then chaired by Lord Nolan stated in their third Report that planning obligations were "the most intractable aspect of the planning system with which we have had to deal . . . (and that they) have a tremendous impact on public confidence." They were informed that such obligations were being used to enable planning permissions to be bought and sold and that developers were being held to ransom and asked to provide benefits which had little or nothing to do with the development proposed. In the Committee's view the evidence they had received made clear that these criticisms were valid. The Committee recommended that the present legislation should be

changed to prevent planning permissions being bought and sold. They also found that the negotiation and terms of planning obligations are sometimes treated as being confidential to the exclusion of those with a legitimate interest in the consideration of the planning application to which they may relate. (1998, 5)

Summary

The current situation as regards contributions to infrastructure costs is obviously unsatisfactory, despite the attempted clarification of replacing the term *planning gain* with *planning obligation*. This gives cause for fresh thinking, including some recent aspirations from the British government. We review these initiatives in Chapter 13 and Appendix C, presenting proposals for legislation and practice designed to avoid previous shortcomings and pave the way to a more acceptable future for LVT in its broadest applications.

PART THREE

Opportunities for Future Land Value Taxation

CHAPTER NINE

LVT in Principle: Criteria for Choosing Options

In Part III, we explore ways that LVT might be implemented in Britain in the future. In this chapter, we consider various criteria for choosing a method of LVT that could be introduced. Our list of criteria, drawn from examples from other countries and from past practical valuation experiments nearer home, provides a starting point from which to derive workable LVT proposals for present-day Britain. In recalling the successes and failures of introducing LVT, as enumerated in Parts I and II, we must keep in mind George Santayana's pointed aphorism: "Those who cannot remember the past are condemned to repeat it."

World Survey

Andelson in his survey (1997, 9) presents a formidably long list of countries where LVT in some form is, or has been, used: Argentina, Canada, Chile, Jamaica and other Caribbean states (Barbados, Belize and Montserrat), the United States, Denmark, Finland, Germany, Hungary, certain East African nations (Kenya, Malawi, Tanzania, Uganda, Zambia and Zimbabwe), South Africa, Abu Dhabi, Hong Kong, Singapore, Japan, South Korea, Papua New Guinea, Australia and New Zealand. He points out, however, that the degree to which LVT is actually used around the world is too slight to provide definitive data, and there is a paucity of hard empirical evidence for its success in practice. Yet, Andelson argues the evidence that does exist is consistent, and its cumulative weight, if not entirely conclusive, is at least impressive.

In his latest edition, Andelson (2000, 97, 129, 205, 239) adds Colombia, Estonia, Great Britain and Mexico to his list, but he still maintains that the implementation of LVT overall has been extremely modest, and its impact, although genuine, has been all too often blunted by countervailing policies, usually at other levels of government; this has been the case particularly in Britain. Despite this realistic acceptance that Georgism has not yet truly arrived,

Andelson is not inhibited from making his peroration to action, as can be seen in an excerpt from the final paragraph of his introduction:

> Like Plato's ideal city, the full Georgist paradigm has been realised nowhere on earth. Only in pale and evanescent glimmerings here and there may faint terrestrial traces of its lineaments be glimpsed. But it remains a steady vision in the heavens. It is not, as in the *Republic*, too sublime for human nature, necessitating a "second-best" substitute like the city of Plato's Laws, better adapted to man's frailty; rather, it is eminently applicable to the problematic human situation. (Andelson 2000, xl)

Andelson here voices the hopes of the Georgist fundamentalists, claiming some measure of success for Georgism around the world, but with the proviso "better sober realism than naïve complacency." He also clearly expresses impatience that the full Georgist paradigm is not widely established as a living and working reality.

But from our research standpoint, in light of more than 100 years of history of attempts at implementing LVT in Britain, together with our understanding of current political prospects, it seems that the argument for gradualism is a more realistic approach (Connellan 2002b).

Definitions of Land Value

McCluskey and Franzsen (2001) explain, in their review of LVT at the local-government level in South Africa, Kenya, Australia, New Zealand and Jamaica, that when values are assigned to land, the definition of land value must mirror the market within which the property is traded. One of the major issues affecting LVT assessments has been the variety of definitions of land value that have been applied. Essentially, three terms are used interchangeably: site value, land value and unimproved value. Each of the jurisdictions examined by McCluskey and Franzsen defines these terms, and, generally speaking, land value and site value are much closer together in their meaning and interpretation. Land value and site value are normally taken to mean the value of the undeveloped land based on highest and best use and assuming that all adjacent infrastructure is in place. Unimproved value is the value of the land in its original condition (marsh, forest, etc.). However, due to its hypothetical nature, the use of unimproved value as a standard for LVT is now declining, and more reliance is being placed on site value. Clearly, a realistic and concise definition of land value is needed in order to provide a defensible assessment.

Prospects for the Basis of Appraisal

Mass appraisal approaches are now seen as an essential element of the appraisal process. They involve valuation of many properties as of a given date, using standard procedures and statistical testing (IAAO 1990, 88). Land value systems would tend to facilitate this approach more readily than other systems by virtue of the fact that fewer variables need to be collected (Fibbens 1995, 61–67). Australia, New Zealand and several states in South Africa have developed computer-assisted mass appraisal systems (CAMA) (McCluskey and Adair 1997, 211). Essential to any mass appraisal procedure is having access to quality data; inherent within this is a process of quality control (Gloudemans 2000, 20).

There is little doubt that geographic information systems (GIS) will have a significant impact on the mass appraisal process, by facilitating more frequent and regular revaluations. One other clearly evident aspect is the need to standardize valuation practices throughout a country via one central assessment body, as in Jamaica, New Zealand and Australia. This has distinct advantages in maintaining standards and in ensuring that equity issues are appropriately addressed.

New approaches to land valuation have also been considered by German et al. (2000, 4–5), particularly from experience gained in Lucas County, Ohio (which includes the city of Toledo), where they have determined that sophisticated and less expensive GIS technology can be used for full integration with CAMA for spatial analysis. Using the same research source in Lucas County, Ward et al. (2002, 15–48) reported further to the International Association of Assessing Officers (IAAO) on the assessment industry's need to integrate CAMA econometric modelling with the geospatial analysis capabilities of GIS.

Revaluations

One of the most important features of any property tax system is its ability to keep value assessments in line with open market values. A failure to regularly revalue creates inequities and distorts the distribution of the tax burden, with correspondingly large changes following any future revaluations. McCluskey and Franzsen (2001, 74–76) confirm that, as a general principle, systems based on LVT tend not to be as volatile as systems based on improved value, because LVT ignores increases in value due to improvements. However, it is important that changes in land values due to market movements, rezoning and highest and best use need to be reflected with an appropriate frequency of revaluations. In the U.K., the lack of revaluations over past decades has given rise to serious assessment and administration problems, discussed in Chapter 4.

Two-Rate Property Taxation in the U.S.

Hartzok describes the experiences of Pennsylvania's cities with two-rate taxation. A standard property tax is actually comprised of two types of taxes, one on building values, and the other on land values. The two types have very different impacts on incentives and development results:

> Pennsylvania's pioneering approach to property tax reform recognizes this important distinction between land and building values through what is known as the split-rate or two-tier property tax. The tax is decreased on buildings, thereby giving property owners the incentive to build and to maintain and improve their properties, and the levy on land values is increased, thus discouraging land speculation and encouraging infill development. This shifting of the tax burden promotes a more efficient use of urban infrastructure (such as roads and sewers), decreases the pressure towards urban sprawl, and assures a broader spread of the benefits of development to the community as a whole. (1997, 205–206)

Hartzok comments also, on the need for a gradual transition process:

> There is a lesson here in the "art of tax improvement." It is necessary to move to the two-rate system while maintaining a revenue neutral tax base, at least initially. Another key is to move gradually. One generally accepted guideline is to shift no more than 20% of the taxes off buildings and onto land each year for a period of five years, or 10% each year for a period of ten years, in order to fully shift all taxes off buildings and onto land value.
>
> Such a gradual transition, combined with community education, allows the citizenry to make the adjustments required, particularly to orient away from expectations of speculative gain in real estate land price escalation and towards investment in the development of affordable housing and business activities. Obviously, as buildings are taxed less their value might rise, while the value of the more heavily taxed land should fall. While more research of these types of effects is needed it would appear from the longer continuation of this tax policy in areas that have tried it that it meets with voter approval. (1997, 212)

In relation to the progress of two-rate taxation in Pennsylvania, Oates and Schwab (1997, 5–19) have researched the impact of urban land taxation on the city of Pittsburgh. They found that in 1978–1980 the city restructured its property tax system by raising the rate on land to more than five times the rate on structures. In the 1980s Pittsburgh experienced a dramatic increase in building activity, far in excess of other cities in the region. Their analysis suggests that, while a shortage of commercial space was a primary driving force behind the expansion, the reliance on increased land taxation played an important supporting role by enabling the city to avoid increases in other taxes that would have impeded development. This conclusion, they argue, is fully consistent with the traditional view that LVT is neutral and that it "provides city officials with a tax instrument that generates revenues but has no damaging side effects on the urban economy. In this way, it allows the city to avoid reliance on other taxes that can undermine urban development" (Oates and Schwab 1997, 19). The political difficulties accompanying long-delayed revaluations led to a repeal of two-rate taxation in Pittsburgh, although it continues in a number of small Pennsylvania cities (Connellan 2001b).

Reviewing Options for the U.K.

We now consider a framework in which to derive a workable proposal for LVT in present-day Britain. In discussing the range of options for implementing LVT, some basic questions arise: Why is such a tax to be imposed? What are the intended achievements and objectives? How does LVT help further these objectives? Are there better ways to achieve the same ends?

Political Pressures

Imposing a land value tax clearly has to be a political decision. But what is the thinking behind it? Is policy guided by political idealism or by pragmatic opportunism? Is the decision in advance of public opinion, or is it trailing it?

Ethical Considerations

Is the LVT designed in line with a political philosophy aimed at distributing wealth by equalising incomes ("from him who hath to him who hath not")? In such a context, are all landowners (at whom the tax is to be targeted) to be equated among the "haves" for the benefit of all nonowners, who are classified as deserving recipients? It is interesting that, in order to support the LVT proposals in the Finance Act of 1910, landowners were practically demonised in Parliament by then Chancellor of the Exchequer (and later Prime Minister) Lloyd George, who equated them with the hated "colliery [coal mine] owners" in his arguments comparing wealth and income derived from land ownership with that from coal mines (Prest 1981, 72, 109, 123).

In the course of the prolonged debates on this Finance Act, Winston Churchill, speaking in support of the Liberal government's proposals, said:

> The landlord who happens to own a plot of land on the outskirts of a great city . . . watches the busy population around him making the city larger, richer, more convenient . . . and all the while sits still and does nothing. Roads are made . . . services are improved . . . water is brought from reservoirs one hundred miles off in the mountains and—all the while the landlord sits still. . . . To not one of these improvements does the landlord monopolist contribute and yet by every one of them the value of his land is enhanced. . . . At last the land becomes ripe for sale—that means the price is too tempting to be resisted any longer. . . . In fact you may say that the unearned increment . . . is reaped by the land monopolist in exact proportion not to the service, but to the disservice done. (Quoted in Hagman and Misczynski 1978, 17–18)

Churchill, in the same debate, said, "the unearned income derived from land arises from a wholly sterile operation" (Hansard 1909).

But to return to our examination of ethical considerations, if the benefit of the tax is to accrue to the "community," who or what is exactly intended by this aspiration? And will its definition vary according to the particular attributes of the tax in question?[1]

Economic Considerations

Henry George (1879, 153–161) argues that landowners have no rights to such ownership (of the land itself, excluding improvements), and thus the community should benefit by 100 percent taxation of those rights, without dire economic repercussions: "[T]he value that attaches to land itself is a value arising from the growth of the community, and can be taken to the last penny without the slightest degree lessening the incentive to production."

But what are the equity perceptions in such deprival by taxation when the existing landowner has acquired these rights by purchasing them in good faith for market value and without prior warning of impending confiscatory process? (Prest 1981, 28)

Raising Revenue

The main reason for introducing LVT could be as straightforward as to raise revenue to augment local or central government coffers. It could be an entirely additional tax or substitute partially or wholly for other taxes.

For Local or National Benefit?

Is LVT to be a local tax for local purposes (which might influence local land policy), or is it to be administered on the national level, for the benefit of the wider community?

Value Capture of Development Gains

Land value can be captured by way of a development gains tax (see Chapter 13) on an "occasion of change," which is a quite different procedure from a site value rate that is levied annually. The political reasoning behind such capital value impositions varies, but it is likely a response to a public perception that landowners are undeservedly reaping large profits from rising land values.

Town Planning

Another political reason to impose LVT could be to fashion or promote a certain type of land use. Georgists have long contended that LVT on the basis of highest and best use will encourage development at the right time in the right place by, for instance, penalising owners of vacant sites for withholding those sites from the market for speculative reasons (Wilks 1964, 11). In contrast, other

---

1. Prest (1981, 127, 182) considers the definition of *community* and illustrates how its ambiguity can obscure the issues.

landowners might be partially or wholly exempted from LVT in the encouragement or pursuit of ecological conservation policies.

Wider Aspects of Taxation Policy

Robertson (1998a) advocates introducing higher taxes and charges on the use of common resources, particularly energy and land, and reducing and perhaps eventually abolishing taxes and charges on employment, income, profit, added value and capital. Such advocacy aims to shift the burden of taxation away from the producers of wealth and towards the nonproductive elements. LVT could play a part in this wider process.

Choices: Variants of LVT Applications

Trigger Mechanisms

The design and ambit of LVT requires choosing which way to apply the tax; this choice may be influenced or even dictated by the initial policy decisions previously mentioned. But what mechanisms might be used to initiate the imposition of such taxation? The tax could be introduced upon the occasion of a number of events. For instance, the tax could be applied to certain classes of landowners after a certain day, or it could be levied when certain defined events occur, such as the disposal or demise of an interest in land, the grant of planning permission, the completion of a development project, or a change in the way land is used.

The type of trigger event chosen is inevitably linked with the design and ambit of the LVT. The following paragraphs set out a range of choices between different applications.

Additional tax or complementary? Will the tax run de novo, as a brand-new, additional tax, or will it run alongside existing land taxes, in partial or complete substitution? For example, could an existing rating system based on the annual value of combined hereditaments of land and buildings be split into two separate taxes, chargeable at different rates, as in some cities in Pennsylvania (Hartzok 1997, 212)?

Valuation base. Is the basis of land valuation for assessment purposes to be existing use—which the Expert Committee on Compensation and Betterment (Uthwatt 1942, 138) describes as "the value of the site as actually developed at the date of each valuation" following the *rebus sic stantibus* rule of the extant rating system—or is it to be the value of the highest and best use that can be reasonably envisaged?

Plan-led or market-led? If land is to be valued on its highest and best use, which would include projecting the land's development value, is this valuation to be strictly plan-led, governed by indications of future use in the approved development plan (see Chapter 14), or is it to take into account the additional influence of market indications of "hope value," irrespective of any firm development plan proposals or approved planning application?

Valuation method. Should the land valuation method be targeted at the capital value of sites or at their annual value? If the latter, can the annual value of land be appraised from direct rental evidence, or does it have to be derived from capital values by a decapitalising process? And is sufficient data available for assessment purposes?

Impact: One-off hit or continuous assessment? Is the assessment a year-by-year tax that continues for the foreseeable future, or is it a one-time charge, based on certain events predetermined by government? The latter process normally focuses on capturing the difference between two capital values (usually with and without the potential of development value), and it relates to actual realisations of such value differences rather than estimated accruals. As we have seen, development gains taxation is usually classified as a one-off operation that occurs upon the occasion of a particular act of development, but value can be captured by other LVT means on an accruals basis, independent of realisation (see Chapter 12).

But what we are also highlighting here is a fundamental difference between two types of LVT, namely site value rating (SVR)—an annual, ongoing tax—and development value capture taxes. In Chapter 10 we set out proposals that address the possibility of running these two types of land value taxes in tandem.

Single or multiple valuation baselines? Is the tax to be derived from a single-stance valuation or from different valuation baselines? For example, LVT could be based at a recurring fixed annual percentage (say 1 percent) of the capital value of a site at its highest and best use, or the tax could be levied at the time that planning permission is granted for development, and based on the difference between the site's value with the benefit of the consent and its value without it. Another possibility would be a continuous tax on the site's incremental value (on a ground rental basis) over a base valuation as of a certain day, and these levels of value could be directed either to its existing use, as envisaged by Uthwatt (1942, 136); to its highest and best use; or to a combination of the two—one eventually melding into the other as a form of gradualism. It is interesting to note that Uthwatt (1942) only went so far as to recommend an annual levy of 75 percent on assessed ground rents on an incremental basis only and related to existing-use site values; details of this Uthwatt scheme are provided in Chapter 10 (Annexe 5).

Level of taxation. If a land tax were levied at a rate equal to 100 percent of net income accruing (including capital gains), there would be no inducement whatsoever to hold land as an asset, either for the sake of current income or for capital appreciation (Hicks 1959, 242; Prest 1981, 38–39; Andelson 1997, 3). A 100 percent tax on ground rent of land at its highest and best use could very well confiscate the whole of a site's value and distort the land market entirely. Some amelioration of such draconian impact would seem prudent (see Chapter 10).

Who pays? Most arguments over LVT are about whether it is fair to the landowners. But some consideration should be given to equation theory. In Britain, tenants currently commit to a certain amount of rent as well as rates, since the extant property tax falls on the occupier, not the landowner. If the tenant were relieved of the rates bill, this could be argued to be only a short-term gain to the tenant, as eventually the tenant would have more money available to pay the owner in rent. In such circumstances, if additional rent accrued to the owner, some of it could be allocated to the site value; consequently, the LVT assessment, as an annual impost, would change to reflect this increase, and the owner's taxation position would not improve. If the owner pays LVT, and the tenant is paying a full market rent that reflects those circumstances, the owner's LVT liability (as existing or as heightened in the future) could not be passed on to the tenant.

A concomitant question is how to impose and distribute a land value tax if there is a hierarchy of leasehold and sub-leasehold interests on a particular property (see Chapter 10). Another analogous example is how to apportion income tax liability from imputed Schedule A (income tax) assessments.

Cushioning LVT (gradualism). Prest (1981, 170) warns of the danger of being too precipitate in introducing LVT. To heed that advice, various cushioning devices could be introduced to ameliorate the effects of LVT:

- exemptions (e.g., agricultural, private housing, etc.);
- incremental levies (Uthwatt 1942);
- current values as against potential values (or moving gradually from one to another);
- indexation of gains or increments (from a base date, as with capital gains tax);
- direct amelioration via selected tax breaks, etc., on targeted uses (e.g., charitable and amenity uses), in accordance with land policy objectives;
- gradually moving from increases on current value increments to potential value increments; and

- equilibrium values as if the tax thereon were payable, in anticipation of full capitalisation—termed by Prest (1981, 37–38) as some sort of Chinese puzzle (but mathematically solvable!).

Interdependence of the Various Land Taxes

In this process of reviewing options for LVT, we need to recognise that all of the various taxes on land interact with one another and that LVT would affect the level of revenue raised by other land taxes. As mentioned in Chapter 3, in general terms, imposing LVT in some form on land affects the open market value (OMV) of that land, and OMV is at the heart of other land taxes like capital gains and inheritance tax.

Benefits of LVT

What then are the arguable benefits of taxing land value?

- *Economic:* LVT would not affect other taxes (except if the process of capitalising the LVT reduced the value of land, in which case the other taxes that are based on the value of land would be affected). LVT is also a tax that cannot be shifted—the landowner could not pass on the burden of the tax to a tenant, for example, because it is assumed that, in market terms, the tenant is already paying as much rent as is affordable and/or appropriate for the land concerned and therefore could not also undertake his landlord's LVT liability.
- *Efficiency:* LVT would be cheaper, quicker and easier to assess (see Wilks [1974] on his Whitstable surveys). From an administrative viewpoint, it would be easier and cheaper to bill and collect LVT from landowners—there are fewer owners than there are occupiers, and if there were any difficulty in identifying the owner, the demand could be made on the occupier, who would then be entitled to pass on the payment of LVT by deducting it from the rent paid to his landlord (and so on, up through a hierarchy of ownership interests).
- *Effectiveness:* LVT is more effective as a taxation instrument than current rates in Britain for exacting contributions towards government expenditures, because it is a tax on owners rather than on occupiers and because it is a tax on land only, rather than on the combination of land and the buildings and improvements thereon. Furthermore, LVT as an annual tax is an effective means of capturing all those increases in land value, which occur because of community actions and not because of the efforts of landowners.

- *Equity:* The proponents of LVT have long held that taxing landowners on their land values is an equitable means of extracting value capture from wealth and even incomes that have not been earned by those landowners. This value is arguably created by the community in various ways over time, for example, by implementing surrounding facilities and infrastructure, and is something that should and could be recouped for the benefit of the community by way of LVT.

Summary

The above options are certainly not exhaustive, and further investigation will no doubt reveal more, but they do indicate the likely range of choices from which we propose to build a rationale for recommendations for LVT. In our view, what does emerge thus far, in the context of proposals for Britain, is support for the case for gradualism. Any acceptance of new and changed land taxation by politicians and the general public alike will have to be weaned by stealthy progression rather than by challenging confrontation.

CHAPTER TEN

Towards Acceptable LVT Systems for Britain

I n the previous chapter we examined criteria for choosing options for the introduction of LVT into Britain. We now examine prospects for acceptable LVT systems for the U.K.

Background

In reviewing land valuation practices around the world, we are inclined to accept Andelson's view (2000, xxxiv) that implementation of LVT has in reality been extremely modest and that its impact has often been blunted by countervailing policies. So, what lessons emerge from such reviews that can be applied to present circumstances in Britain? One thing is clear: there is a considerable range of options. To start our examination, we look at the extremes, as suggested by Prest (1981, 170).

The "Deep End": The Georgist Approach

The deepest (Georgist) end involves assessing the value of all land at its highest and best use (as interpreted by the market, including hope value in advance of any planning confirmation) and taxing the owner at 100 percent of the full economic rental value. This would be tantamount to government sequestration of the value of the land. Some commentators have made this point in various ways and contexts:

> Were a site's rent to be socially appropriated in full for the foreseeable future, its capital or selling value would be extinguished. (Andelson 2000, xxii)

> [I]f a land tax is levied at a rate equal to 100% of the net income accruing (including capital gains) there would be no inducement whatever to hold land as an asset either for the sake of any current income or for capital appreciation reasons. In these circumstances, speculative land holding would be pointless. (Prest 1981, 38–39)

So what would be the point of owning land, other than for occupation? An owner in occupation would pay a quasi-rent, by way of taxation, to some level of government. There would be no real investment market as such in land itself; no freeholder could lease the land at a rent, as this would all be swallowed up by land tax. Nor could the freeholder sell his interest as an investment, because there would be no positive cash flow, and it would only be a tax liability. Admittedly, a prospective occupier could be interested in such a scenario of land tax payments, but then only as a quasi-rent, which would be paid to the government, not to the erstwhile freehold owner. The end result would be that, while the government would not have nationalised the land, it would have nationalised the rent in the land without payment of compensation. This would leave owner-occupiers the freedom to invest in improvements and carry on business on the land or simply live there, in return for 100 percent taxes on the land's rental value.

This means that landowners' interests would be liquidated by taxation, and even owner-occupiers, paying LVT in lieu of rent, would feel the financial pinch if their use of the land were anything less than the highest and best use value assigned by the market. However, this assumes that there would still be a market from which to extract such values—a doubtful premise on which to base an LVT system.

Since the process would really be the nationalisation of rental value and the right to receive it, this has to be compared with the extant British system of nationalising development rights and holding them, in escrow-like fashion, until the time comes for obtaining planning permission, with no compensation for refusal of permission and no betterment levy for approval except for buying into the extant planning gain or planning obligation (see Chapter 8).

Away from the Deepest End

Short of the full Georgist solution, a whole range of possibilities for LVT exists:

1. Land is assessed based on full economic rental values (including hope values), but the rate applied is less than 100 percent, ensuring that some semblance of ownership of rental value rights is maintained and that the land market survives.

2. Under the same conditions as (1), values are allocated only to highest and best uses that are plan-led, i.e., in line with development plan expectations. This was the amended basis adopted by Wilks (1974) in his second Whitstable survey in Kent (see Annexe 3 to this chapter for further details).

3. Land is valued separately from buildings and other improvements, and different rates of tax are allocated to each. This is at the heart of the Pennsylvania two-rate system as reviewed by Hartzok (1997).

4. In order to deal with political opposition, instead of taxing all land and all landowners the same way across the board, there could be certain exemptions from such an all-embracing tax, e.g., agricultural interests, ownerships having charitable and cultural significance, or residential property (which would have considerable political influence). Selective taxation could even be a way to encourage land policy aspirations.

5. Instead of basing the tax on the full current value of the site, the tax could be raised incrementally: it would only apply to excess values beyond a valuation base date. This principle was recommended by Uthwatt (1942), but it is important to recall that his committee was only considering taxing incremental existing-use values of land and not highest and best values. But even if land were taxed based on highest and best use, this option still might be politically attractive, because existing owners would retain the land value that they already owned, regardless of any future taxes on incremental gains.

6. Land taxation could be based on current existing use, which would eschew some of the fundamental arguments for LVT in encouraging development and penalising land hoarding.

Each of these options would affect the land market differently. The deepest end would result in the drastic outcomes outlined by Andelson and Prest. A smaller market impact would result from the less-extreme options. Prest (1981, 37–39) illustrates this phenomenon with a series of examples showing the effects of differing rates of LVT on a capital value base. As land taxation rates increase, capital values decrease, and when the rate reaches 100 percent, there is no inducement to hold land itself as an investment asset, although there could be some incentive for investing in buildings and other improvements on the land.

Some Obstacles to Introducing LVT

There are, of course, arguable obstacles to introducing LVT, even at the shallow end. Valuation of land could be difficult, and revaluation might be expensive; aborting existing local revenue tax systems could be costly and disruptive; and tracing landowners and apportioning their tax liability throughout the hierarchy of possible legal interests that may subsist within an individual land holding could be extremely difficult, as has been pointed out:

> The serious question, and the one which has been the subject of most controversy, is the division of the site value rate between the owners of interests superior to that of the occupier. (Turvey 1957, 79)

> [E]ven if one can disentangle the total value of a site by some means, the apportionment of tax liability between a freeholder and a lessee may be a source of further difficulty, unless one imposes the whole of the tax at one level and allows the different interests to sort it out between them. But that has been held to be a Draconian situation. (Prest 1981, 42)

However, a remedy that would appeal less to Draco, and perhaps more to Solon, is worth considering in an effort to disentangle such difficulties in tracing owners and allocating the tax burden among hierarchical land interests (see Annexe 4 to this chapter).

The Deep or Shallow End?

Putting all of these different strands together, what sort of LVT legislation and practice would be compatible with Britain's town and country planning system? LVT should accomplish the following objectives:

- garner government revenues in a fairer and more comprehensive way;
- capture development value for the benefit of the community; and
- support plan-led land policy (encouraging the right development at the right time in the right place and discouraging wrong development).

The present Labour government, following the previous Labour administration, has demonstrated a disinclination to overtly rock the financial boat. As far as local government revenues are concerned, the administration has shown reluctance to amend the council tax banding basis, which is still manifestly regressive, and it has put off any prospect of a revaluation for this particular tax until 2007 (see Chapter 4). Although government went ahead with a revaluation of nondomestic properties for business rates for the year 2000, and it will again in 2005, the existing basic principle that the uniform business rate (UBR) is set nationally, not locally, is likely to be retained, as confirmed by DETR (1988b). Taking a cautionary stance into account, and realising that any steps towards a new property tax scheme would be unlikely to emerge until further into the current Labour government's term of office (and perhaps even beyond), the shallowest end seems the best place to fish for possible LVT solutions.

In this vein, it is relevant to recap what such a solution should do:

- make the system fairer (equity rules!);
- move forward slowly, gradually and experimentally;
- not rock the boat or make too many waves for the government; and
- identify and tax land profits.

Prest argues that it is possible for an LVT (or site value rating) system to run alongside a generic development gains tax system. Regarding the latter, he suggests that there is no point in going beyond a special form of capital gains tax (CGT) targeting land deals, perhaps with:

- a higher-than-normal rate of CGT;
- no rollovers (i.e., postponing the tax liability from an initial disposal and repurchase until a subsequent disposal takes place); and
- increased taxation opportunities, perhaps on points of accrual, and not restricted to acts of disposal (but this would involve periodic valuation processes, which could prove cumbersome and expensive). (Prest 1981, 176–177)

Apart from such special tax hits on the potential profit takers from land deals (see Chapter 12), there is the question of whether to tax land annually in order to garner government revenues. We evaluate this question in terms of a system that might favour this type of tax and in terms of the general acceptance of such taxation in government and in wider circles.

Over time, with regular and periodic revaluations, such an annual tax will gradually gear itself to the accumulating value of land from whatever cause. So, we now examine what is essentially an SVR system for Britain: an annual tax to replace extant rates (property taxes).

A Simple Solution?

Complexities and implementation costs of previous LVT attempts in Britain have largely contributed to their failure, therefore, any recommended system must be comparatively simple for it to have any chance of success (Connellan 1998). Gradualism, or changing taxation procedures in stages, seems to make more sense and to be more likely to be accepted than any dramatic overnight replacement of existing property taxation procedures.

Within this context, we put forward the following scheme:

- The trigger events would be the revaluations of nondomestic properties for rating, which take place quinquennially in 2005 and 2010.
- The government's Inland Revenue Valuation Agency would make an apportionment of the assessments of total property annual value between its components of land (site) value and the value attributable to buildings, etc. Initially, both values would be derived from existing uses, on the principle of *rebus sic stantibus* (see Chapter 4 and Uthwatt 1942, 139).
- The annual land value would thus become the basis of the owner's land tax (a form of site value rating), and the annual value for buildings, etc., would become the basis of the occupier's rate. Differing taxation rates

could be applied according to the policies of central and local governments, following Pennsylvania's two rates approach.

- The combined tax liability would be met in the first instance by the "rating occupier" (the tenant), but the amount of the owner's land tax could be deducted from the rent that the occupier paid to the immediate landlord. Thereafter, the owner's tax burden could be passed upward and apportioned throughout a hierarchical chain of successive owners' interests (see further discussion in Annexe 4; see also Annexe 6 and Appendix B on the practicalities of introducing SVR as an annual tax to eventually replace the extant rates system).

Towards a More Comprehensive Form of LVT

The above proposals reflect the dual-rate taxing of land and buildings, being separately targeted on existing uses or, as Uthwatt puts it, "the annual value of the site as then actually and physically developed and as if it were permanently restricted against any other form of development" (1942, 139). But consideration would also have to be given to properties outside the present rating system, for example, agricultural holdings (particularly on the urban fringes), vacant sites and derelict property (see Chapter 4 for details of rating exemptions). This political decision would be fairly bold, but if it were decided to extend the taxation net and to embrace the long-argued merits of LVT in influencing land policy, it would be possible to assess such land on the basis of highest and best use on plan-led principles and to tax the owners directly alongside the dual-rate system described above. For the details that would be required for such a valuation exercise in Britain, we can return to Wilks (1974) and the bases he adopted in his experiments at Whitstable in Kent (see Annexe 3).

But moving towards a more comprehensive form of LVT, at some later time it would be possible to reassess the annual land element from the dual-rate assessment and thereafter base the owner's land tax not on the land's existing use but on its highest and best use (as defined by plan-led principles), while still retaining the occupier's assessment on existing buildings and improvements. The dual-rate system might run for a while on this basis, but it would then be just a short technical step to drop the occupier's assessment altogether and tax the owner solely on the land's highest and best use value. Both of these adjustments of valuation and tax bases could be cushioned by transitional steps over a period of time, if politically and socially appropriate.

But the actual method of collecting the owner's progressing tax liability could be that the identified rateable occupier initially could pay the owner's tax and then deduct it from the rent they paid to the immediate (lowest-order) landlord, and so on upwards through any chain of ownership interests (see Annexe 4). However, by the time the occupier's assessment was superseded, the immediate owner would have become readily identifiable, and the owner's tax demand could be redirected accordingly.

Council Tax

Might LVT also be applied to domestic properties? Because house owners now contribute to local government revenues via the council tax, the present Labour government may well be reluctant to move towards LVT on domestic properties, which would be a drastic change. However, it is still pertinent for the future to examine how LVT considerations could be incorporated into the council tax system. In particular, if allocation into value bands, rather than discrete property valuations, is the norm, how could apportionments between the value of land and the value of buildings and other improvements be made?

In the face of such constraints, any solution would need to take a relatively broad-brush approach to the valuation process. Apportionments to land value could probably only be made within the existing value bands on across-the-board percentage bases: within a particular rating area, certain percentages could be prescribed for the various value bands. This would approximate the constituent land value element and pave the way to a dual-rate tax system, analogous to the nondomestic system previously described.

With some forward thinking from tax administrators and assessors, the same trail towards LVT could be followed with respect to collecting and apportioning tax liabilities throughout a hierarchy of landowners. Similarly possible is an eventual shift towards a single land tax based on highest and best use for domestic properties, within the constraints of the extant planning system. However, as with the proposals for nondomestic properties, the speed and extent of such progressions would have to be measured against political and social expediency.

Agricultural Land

Agricultural land and buildings have long been exempt from rating liability in Britain (General Rate Act of 1967 and Rating Act of 1971). If such liability were to be reintroduced, LVT could arguably be the simplest way forward: most assessments could be levied on agricultural value as utilised. However, with properties such as urban fringe land, where the approved development plan reflects development expectations, the assessment would be based on the land's highest and best use, which in this case would be its plan-led use, rather than on its current agricultural use.

Although such assessment procedures would follow Georgist precepts of equity and fairness, the current hardships claimed for the agricultural industry would again mean that political and social expediency would significantly affect the timing of introducing such measures.

Commentary on the Proposed Scheme

According to the proposal, an owner's LVT would be introduced after a quinquennial revaluation by splitting the latest nondomestic rating assessments between site value and improvements (buildings, etc.). Royal Institution of Chartered Surveyors (1995)[1] gives some advice in Guidance Note 5 (GN 5) on the process of apportioning, which has been previously commented upon by Britton et al. (1991, 161–67), and the relevant parts of this commentary are reproduced in Annexe 5a (www.lincolninst.edu).

Although the above guidance to valuers is directed towards apportionments of capital values for accounting purposes, it is not a quantum leap for rating practitioners to also adapt such recommended methods to apportioning annual values. Of course some changes would have to be made in the processes of apportioning large-scale undertakings currently assessed by the profits method or by statutory formulas. However, with some ingenuity, which has never been in short supply in the rating valuation profession, the outcome certainly need not be one of insurmountable difficulties (Connellan et al. 1998).[2]

Alternative Initial Approaches

Lichfield and Connellan (2000a) proposed that nonrated land should be taxed at an appropriate percentage rate on a full LVT value based on highest and best use, in accordance with the development plan. This might well now be challengeable as discriminatory, however, as other (rated) owners are initially to be taxed on the basis of land value related to existing use. A possible remedy would be to tax these unrated owners initially on a matching existing use basis or, alternatively, on an incremental basis (Uthwatt 1942), following Uthwatt precepts but geared to highest and best use values rather than existing use values. This would mean establishing a base date (for example, the next rating revaluation in 2005) and taxing property owners thereafter on the yearly increments in their land value at an assessed percentage tax (see Annexe 5), but related to highest and best use in accordance with development plan proposals.

However, it would only be a partial tax hit on development rights, which are now actually in the ownership of the Crown.

Transitional Stages

The process of developing land will, of course, bring nonrated land into the net of apportioned rating assessments, and the land value thus determined will reflect the degree to which the owner chose to develop (or not develop) the land

---

1. This manual is currently under revision, but similar advice is being retained.

2. It is interesting and relevant to note that Uthwatt proposed virtually the same procedure of apportioning the annual values of land and buildings as part of the rating assessment process without any concern over its practicability (Uthwatt 1942, 137).

up until the time of the assessment. This development and rating process will subsume any prior incremental taxation (or fuller taxation) of such previously unrated land.

Eventually, the tax system might move beyond being based on existing use value on rated land and possible incremental value on highest and best use on unrated land. The ultimate goal of a consolidated LVT program based on highest and best use value of all rated and unrated land (at appropriate tax rate percentages) might be on a future government agenda. The effect of any transitions between different valuation and taxation bases on land can be cushioned over time by slowly merging those bases. But as they gradually become capitalised into land market prices (and a downward pressure could be anticipated in real terms), they will in turn tend to affect other fiscal measures that are geared to the land market (e.g., CGT, inheritance tax, income tax, etc.). In addition, it should be remembered that all of the tenets of value capture through LVT itself (planning gains, impact fees, greenfield taxes and the like) over time will tend to work through the capitalisation process to produce ripples in the land market, in what Prest refers to as "a sort of Chinese puzzle argument" (1981, 37).

Responses to Possible Criticisms

- *Apportioning rating assessments between land and buildings could be technically difficult.* Uthwatt has already endorsed the feasibility of the exercise, and the practice is in place in the dual-rate system adopted in Pennsylvania (see also Annexe 5a for technical considerations).
- *Targeting only existing use land values could be seen as merely "scratching the surface."* It is a reasonable starting point and it establishes the principle of an owner's assessment and tax liability on land value. It also provides scope for differential taxation (via different percentage rates) between owners and occupiers and between different types of land use.
- *The scheme is just another form of rating (local property tax).* Initially it lessens the load on the occupier, depending on the lease structure, by transferring some of the tax burden to the owner. It also opens up the possibility of progressing towards a more universal form of LVT, which would affect owners of land currently rated and unrated.
- *The system initially only reaches ratepayers.* Certain proposals encompass unrated land, which could eventually lead to the full valuation assessment of land at highest and best use (levied at appropriate percentage rates).
- *Within the ambit of existing rating valuations, there are "grey areas" that will only achieve minimum assessment for what may be temporary existing uses, e.g., reserve land held for future expansion within an industrial complex or within a statutory formula assessment.* Rating assessments are

derived from hypothetical tenancies on a year-to-year basis and are therefore unlikely to reflect underlying and unrealised development values. However, if the proposed transition is eventually made, and all land is valued on a highest and best use basis, any differential problems, either between the classifications of rated and unrated properties or within those classifications themselves, will be resolved.

• *There is nothing in the scheme for owners.* The intention of LVT is to place the burden on those arguably best able to bear it. But there might be some solace for those taxpayers in Britain who have long been claiming unfairness in the lack of tax write-offs for depreciation of buildings and other improvements. If property owners are clearly taxed on "the indestructibility of the soil," and, in taxation terms, the indestructible part of real estate is considered separately from the parts that are destructible, will not this lend weight to the claims from those same owners for an extension of income and/or corporation tax allowances for depreciation of buildings and other improvements (perhaps on the U.S. pattern)?

Summary

What seems to be emerging from the above, as far as acceptable LVT systems for Britain are concerned, is the possibility of combining an annual impost on land values with a capital levy, perhaps by means of an enhanced capital gains tax. But, we must remember the fundamental differences between two types of LVT: SVR as an annual ongoing tax, and development value capture taxes. Are they mutually exclusive, or can they be imposed side by side? Prest has some interesting and relevant views in support of running the two types of land value taxes:

> Objections of principle are sometimes raised on the grounds that it would be inequitable to have a tax system which includes both taxation of the stock of capital and taxation of the increments in the stock. This point is misconceived. First of all, it is generally accepted today that capital gains are a form of income and that some kind of annual tax should therefore be applied to them as well as to other forms of income. The taxation of wealth separately from and in addition to income is a matter for considerable discussion depending on whether one thinks there is a case for differential taxation on investment income. . . . However, even if one were not convinced of the separateness of wealth taxation and capital gains taxation at the national level, the proposal in question is the combination of the local site value rating with a central DLT (Development Land Tax). If it is considered desirable to have a local source of local finance and some sort of tax on realty as the best way of giving effect to that principle, then it is perfectly reasonable to have the two taxes simultaneously.

> What seems to be behind the incompatibility arguments is the proposition that gains on development amount to a large fraction of land capital values and

so that two taxes would have a very similar base. Even if this proposition were true, it would be incorrect to deduce that one cannot have both kinds of tax operated simultaneously, especially when one is at local and the other at central level.

What is perfectly true is that if both taxes existed simultaneously there would be a number of interactions between them. Thus SVR (Site Value Rating) might be expected to reduce the land values through the capitalization process.... More generally, if the combined burden of local SVR and national DLT, or any other tax on land gains, were thought to be too great an imposition on allocation or distributional grounds, there would be plenty of scope for some sort of crediting arrangements of local SVR against national taxes, as with property taxation in different parts of North America today.... [N]either arguments or general principle nor historical precedent lead to the conclusion that it is impossible to have a combination of the two main types of tax if it is so desired. (1981, 178–179)

As with many other issues, perhaps we should leave Prest with the last words on that particular subject.

■ ANNEXE THREE
Approach to Site Valuation in Britain

In considering how to apply land taxation in Britain, we favour the valuation approach that Wilks used in his two research exercises at Whitstable in 1963 and 1973. In his earlier exercise, Wilks took his guidance from the old London County Council's attempt to introduce site value rating via its L.C.C. Bill (1938–1939), because this measure was considered a well-thought-out example of prospective legislation. However, Wilks did identify some practical difficulties in applying some of the valuation principles enumerated therein, and in his later exercise, he made some important amendments to clarify the task for the valuer and to maximise consistency and acceptability of results.

We therefore prefer Wilks's changes to the scenario and, in particular, his amended definition of value quoted below, which has similarities to the definition we cited in Chapter 3, "land construed for LVT purposes."

> The annual site value of a land unit shall be the annual rent which the land comprising at that land unit might be expected to realize if it demised with vacant possession at the [appointed valuation date] in the open market by a willing lessor on a perpetually renewable tenure upon the assumption that on the [appointed valuation date]
>
> (1) there were no buildings, erection or works on or under the land unit except existing roads adopted by a public authority and existing public utility services;
>
> (2) there were no encumbrances on the land save those registered under the Land Registration Act 1968;
>
> (3) all planning considerations relevant to the development value to be reflected in the annual site value have been taken into account;
>
> (4) subject to (5) below, there were not upon or in that land unit anything growing except grass, heather, gorse, sedge or other natural growth;
>
> (5) in the case of agricultural land, the land was unimproved and in a state and condition such that, under the provision of the Agricultural Acts, neither claim nor counter claim would arise upon a change of occupancy. (Wilks 1975, 8)

As points of further relevance, Wilks tendered the following precepts to any valuer commissioned in a site value rating exercise:

> Certain broad planning policy statements should be ignored by the valuer as they must involve "hope" value and not assist any site value determination as a result

of delegated powers. With all policy statements the valuer must determine as to whether the statement is a "puff" or a solid fact direct affecting the immediate site value. (Wilks 1974, 16)

The valuer is to be totally dispassionate and will disregard deliberately and totally all civil transactions relating to landlords and tenants and all legislation affecting those transactions. (Wilks 1974, 14)

Wilks further comments on the above definition of value, saying that in 1973 he was far more able to base the exercise on the planning situation than he was in 1963:

Thus I have placed less extravagant values for underdeveloped land where there was in effect only hope value. It seemed to me that hope without planning permission was of no value within the definition. Equally, on amenity land, public open space and so on, whereas before I used the compulsory purchase value, I now realize that was wrong in principle and that it should be the value of the land as if it were perpetually restricted to open space purposes and therefore worth considerably less. In this way I was able far more closely to follow the actual planning requirements and the actual permissions on any and every parcel of land.

It is crucial to the valuer to regard positive town planning restrictions as limiting the site user of any site just as much as increasing the potential of underdeveloped sites.

Town planning restrictions will not affect supply and demand unless the restrictions are backed up by Statute, or the equivalent. It is submitted that any statutory "guidance" as to the use and intensity of use of a site amounts to a restrictive covenant on that site.

The valuer's problem is not too easy. If land is designated for development, the position is very clear. There will be many cases where appeal decisions etc. indicate hope for development. We submit it as a matter of fact alone for the valuer to decide whether the evidence proves a site value or whether the evidence should be ignored simply because it indicates "hope" value.

In conclusion the valuer therefore sees "Town Planning" as imposing site restrictions or limitations. The line between hard facts and high hopes is faintly drawn but it is the valuer's duty to value as he sees them, not to prognosticate as a town planner. (1974, 16–17)

■ ANNEXE FOUR

Apportioning Land Value Tax to Hierarchical Owners

This proposed process can best be illustrated by an example of a property (land and buildings) with a hierarchical ownership extending from the freeholder down to the occupying tenant via a ground lessee and an intermediate leaseholder as follows:

- Freeholder grants a 99-year ground lease to Ground Lessee at a rent of £200 per annum (pa).
- Ground Lessee grants a 42-year lease to Lessee at a rent of £1,000 pa.
- Lessee lets to Tenant on an occupational tenancy for 20 years at a rent of £5,000 pa.

Rules for Apportioning Land Value Tax (LVT)

Freehold owner's land tax is set at x% of the assessed annual site value. All tenants and leaseholders can deduct from the rent that they pay to their immediate landlord:

- x% of the assessed annual site value *or*
- x% of the rent that they pay to their landlord,

whichever is *less*.

Land Value Tax Assessment

Land value is assessed at £1,500. At 50 percent rate of tax, the land value tax liability to be apportioned is £750.

Applying the Apportionment Rules

- Occupying tenant pays the initial land value tax of £750 (£1,500 @ 50 percent) to the assessing authority and immediately deducts it from the payment of rent to Lessee. Tenant pays £5,000 minus £750 = £4,250 to Lessee.

- Lessee, receiving the reduced rent of £4,250 from Tenant, can only deduct £500 (£1,000 @ 50 percent) from the payment of rent to Ground Lessee. Lessee pays £500 (£1,000 minus £500) to Ground Lessee.

TABLE 7: Apportioning LVT to Hierarchical Owners

Party	Profit Rent Before Land Value Tax			Profit Rent After Land Value Tax			Reduced Profit Rent
	Rent Received	Rent Paid	Profit Rent	Rent Received	Rent Paid	Profit Rent	LVT Allocation
Tenant	£5,000	£5,000	£0	£4,250	£4,250	£0	£0
Lessee	£5,000	£1,000	£4,000	£4,250	£500	£3,750	£250
Ground Lessee	£1,000	£200	£800	£500	£100	£400	£400
Freeholder	£200	£0	£200	£100	£0	£100	£100
Totals			**£5,000**			**£4,250**	**£750**

- Ground Lessee, receiving the reduced rent of £500 from Lessee, can only deduct £100 (£200 @ 50 percent) from the payment of rent to Freeholder. Ground Lessee pays £100 (£200 minus £100) to Freeholder.

- Freeholder receives the reduced rent of £100.

Consequential Effects of Apportionment

By comparing the before and after situations of each party in relation to their individual profit rents, the distributional pattern of the land value tax can be identified in the schedule of apportionment demonstrated in Table 7. Being taxed here is the right to receive any profit rent that can be ascribed to the land value. As the latter has been assessed at £1,500, the land value tax payable of 50 percent has to be distributed among those who enjoy such land profit rents to the tune of a total land value tax payment of £750.

Somewhat analogous to the above process of distributing LVT liability throughout the ownership chain is the current value added tax, which is collected from consumers in stages throughout the business chain.

■ ANNEXE FIVE

Uthwatt's Betterment Levy Scheme

The following extracts from Uthwatt (1942, 135–154) describe the then recommended scheme as points of reference for latter-day revisiting of those ideas in the main text of this chapter.

Recommended Scheme for Periodic Levy on Increases in Annual Site Values

Outline of Principles

- That, as soon as the necessary legislation is passed, there shall be ascertained the annual site value of every rateable hereditament as actually developed, such value to be a fixed datum line from which to measure all future increases in annual site value. No valuation is to be made in the case of agricultural land and farmhouses.
- That a revaluation should be made every five years of the annual site value as then developed.
- That there should be a levy in each of the five years following each revaluation of a fixed proportion (say 75%) of the amount of any increase in the annual site value over the fixed datum line as revealed by the revaluation.
- That the levy should be borne by the person actually enjoying or capable of realizing the increased value.
- That the necessary valuations should be made through the existing valuation of machinery for ordinary rating purposes, and entered in the rating valuation lists.

Practicalities of Assessment

What the Committee had in mind was that, when the annual values of hereditaments were being arrived at quinquennially in the ordinary course, it should not involve much extra expense to ascertain and record their annual site values at the same time. It recommended, therefore, that in the valuation lists made for rating purposes there should be provided an additional column, in which should be entered quinquennially the annual site value of every hereditament separately assessable for rates.

Conclusion

The following advantages were claimed for the levy scheme:

- The scheme will catch increments arising from the public expenditure, from the operation of the provisions of planning schemes, and from general community causes
- The scheme excludes from levy all increases in the annual value of property due to individual skills and enterprise, and it does not tax improvements
- The scheme does not import hypotheses as to what could be done with the site but is confined to the facts that happen
- The increase in site value will in fact have been realized or enjoyed or will be realizable before becoming subject to the levy
- The use of the existing rating valuation machinery is the most economical way of ascertaining annual site values
- The machinery for local assessment and objection to local valuation lists is already familiar to the public
- **The ascertaining of annual site values will provide a basis for the differential rating of sites and buildings to the relief for improvements (i.e., permitting tax reductions for improvements), should it be desired to introduce such a system.**[3]

---

3. Author's bolding.

■ **ANNEXE SIX**
LVT in Practice

Tony Vickers has conducted research (2000; 2002) that concentrates on the main proposal to introduce site value rating (SVR) as an annual tax to replace the extant rates system (property tax). (The proposals from Chapter 10 that fell outside of SVR were deliberately left out of Vickers's research.) The complete version of Vickers's input is found in Appendix B.

The principle issues in Vickers's research included: the technical and administrative measures necessary for the introduction of this form of LVT; the processes involved; and implementation proposals, including the design and operation of smart-tax pilot schemes in selected parts of the U.K., perhaps coupled with BIDs (business improvement districts), to act as test beds for national adoption of LVT within a suggested time scale.

Vickers's Route Map

Vickers organised a postal survey of property tax stakeholders that tested whether LVT in principle would indeed be acceptable in Britain today. Interviews and correspondence were also conducted with valuation and other experts on the basis that a national land valuation for taxation was both practically and politically possible.

The survey reaffirmed the case for a gradual approach to implementing LVT. Vickers also found an overwhelming degree of ignorance about current systems of governance, property taxation and land information management and strong support for the idea of piloting LVT in one or two areas before making any decision about nationwide implementation.

Technology and Administration

The technology available to make any property tax system more efficient is constantly improving, thanks to geographic information systems (GIS). Britain is well placed to provide, within three to five years, a complete, consistent, accurate and up-to-date set of spatial data objects that represent the totality of the U.K. land mass. In general, technology is both pushing governments away from conventional taxes on mobile transactions and entities and pulling them towards property taxes, especially LVT.

From an administrative standpoint, there is a good case for using pilot programs to devise the best practice in an area of public life that is as complex as property taxation. Over time, static tax assessments can become unfair, which supports the case for frequent reviews.

LVT Processes

The first logical stage in administering LVT is to identify parcels of land and units of tax assessment. The present UBR, based on occupancy, does not require site ownership to be identified, whereas an LVT system would need to.

Two linked processes follow the identification of parcels and owners: physical measurement and assessment of value for tax purposes.

Gradually Improving Administration

If LVT were to be phased in alongside other local taxes, gradually replacing UBR in particular, it would have the administrative advantage of not requiring existing proven systems to be adapted radically. They could be allowed to fade away once LVT was proved to work well.

Starting LVT in just a few areas, using pilots, and at an initial low rate to test new systems would be advantageous to a sudden nationwide change. In pilot areas having a large proportion of vacant and underused land, regeneration effects would also increase the overall property tax take.

Criteria for selecting pilot areas might include:

- status of local authority information systems (especially for land use and economic performance);
- level of economic distress;
- degree of support from business community; and
- "fit" within overall geographic spread of all pilots.

Implementation Proposals

Smart-Tax Option

A smart-tax option is intended to suit areas in need of urban renewal. Vickers recommended that smart-tax pilots be permitted as part of a continuing implementation of Urban Task Force (UTF) fiscal recommendations. Business improvement districts (BIDs) might provide an ideal opportunity to implement smart-tax pilots on a smaller scale.

Vacant Land Tax Before Smart-Tax Pilots

The UTF recommended a vacant land tax (VLT), levied annually, as a highly effective measure to stimulate urban renewal in areas suffering dereliction and blight. It seems appropriate that if government announces its intention to introduce LVT and invites pilot smart-tax bids, it should also announce that it will first introduce a VLT for the whole U.K.

Summary

We propose a gradual approach, and we suggest that this whole range of measures (local, regional and national LVT) may take 15 years to introduce.

CHAPTER ELEVEN

Future Recoupment via Ownership

W e now consider the prospects for implementing LVT in the form of value capture opportunities, the first of which is recoupment via ownership: virtually a process of land banking by public authorities, usually in advance of long-term development proposals, thus pre-empting the accrual of value for the benefit of the community (Grant 1999, 62).

Compulsory-Acquisition Difficulties

The compulsory purchase order (CPO) process (eminent domain in the U.S.), as a means of ensuring land assembly from fragmented ownership in all cases where voluntary negotiation fails, has limitations. A report commissioned by the Department of the Environment, Transport and the Regions from the City University (DETR 1997c) identified the following difficulties:

- lengthy time scales;
- user dissatisfaction with the CPO process and outcome;
- problems with the current dispute-resolution procedures in the CPO process;
- the blighting effect of CPOs that are not implemented;
- the conflict-ridden nature of the CPO process; and
- the resistance of a very high proportion of local authorities to the use of CPO powers.

Follow-up Events to the City University Report
Review by DETR

In June 1998 the DETR instituted a fundamental review of the laws and procedures relating to compulsory purchase, compensation and the disposal of compulsorily purchased land. An advisory group, whose membership embraced the spectrum of professional competence and relevant interests, published an interim report (DETR 1999a) containing recommendations for wider dissemination and discussion; a final report (DETR 2000b) was issued in July 2000.

The main thrust of the findings was to confirm that the current compulsory purchase arrangements are basically sound and that there are adequate safeguards to protect the rights of those whose property is taken away from them. However, it was recognised that the existing legislative base is complex and convoluted, and the review therefore recommended consolidating, codifying and simplifying the law, preparing new compulsory purchase and compensation legislation, and bringing it before Parliament at the earliest opportunity. The report also recommended that the open market value of land should remain the normal basis for determining the compensation payable for the land taken.

Law Commission

In December 2000, following discussion with the Law Commission, the DETR and the Lord Chancellor's Department approved terms of reference for a preliminary study to identify the likely features of a project to take on board the government's intended review of reported difficulties in the existing compulsory purchase system. Subsequently, the Law Commission published a preliminary report, which stated:

> There is general agreement that current law and practices are cumbersome and convoluted. The long lead-time not only generates uncertainty and financial loss for the current landowners but it also makes the procedure unattractive to potential investors as a means of assembling land for major infrastructure or regeneration schemes. (Law Commission 2001, 1)

The Law Commission made it clear that its paper was in line with the conclusions of the DETR review and assumed the preservation of the principal features of the existing system together with improvements.

Planning Green Paper

Following the above initiatives, the government published a discussion document entitled *Planning Green Paper: Planning Delivering a Fundamental Change* (ODPM 2001) that invited comments on certain planning proposals, including compulsory purchase and compensation. The government later published its response to these invited comments (ODPM 2002a), which confirmed certain main proposals (relevant to this chapter) that are to be followed up by the government:

- further collaboration with the Law Commission to reform the law on compensation and implementation in order to introduce "clear, unambiguous, consolidated and codified legislation";
- greater powers to be given to local planning authorities to enable them to acquire land for the purpose of carrying out "development, redevelopment or improvement which they consider will be for the economic, social and/or environmental benefit of its area"; and

- additional compensation to owners and occupiers of acquired properties
  as affected by compulsory-purchase orders "by providing for an additional
  'loss payment' in recognition of the compulsory nature of the acquisition."

Planning and Compulsory Purchase Bill

Part 7 of the Planning and Compulsory Purchase Bill, introduced in the House
of Commons in December 2002, deals with the reform of the compulsory purchase system as set out in the government's green papers mentioned above.[1] It
amends the existing power of local authorities, joint planning boards and National
Park authorities under section 226(1)(a) of the Town and Country Planning Act
of 1990 to compulsorily acquire land that is suitable for and required in order to
secure the carrying out of development, redevelopment or improvement. Local
authorities will be able to acquire land by compulsory purchase if they think that
it will facilitate the carrying out of development, redevelopment or improvement
on or in relation to the land, on condition that such acquisition will be of economic, social or environmental benefit to their area. Part 7 also makes provision
for a new statutory scheme, which, subject to certain exceptions, provides for
additional "loss payments" for owners and occupiers not entitled to receive
payments under the home loss scheme set out in sections 29–33 of the Land
Compensation Act of 1973.

Effect on Compensation Levels for Land Taken

There have been no fundamental changes in the general level of compensation
for land compulsorily acquired, apart from the additional loss payments proposed
above. As described in Chapter 6, the Land Compensation Act of 1961 provided
that compensation shall be the market value of the land, subject to the modification that the acquiring authority shall not pay any increase or decrease in the
land's value if it was brought about by the development scheme that prompted
the compulsory purchase (Heap 1996, 330). Thus, the scope for recoupment of
development value via purchase for ownership under compulsory-purchase rules
is limited to any increase in value between the land's market value with the benefit of the development scheme and without the benefit of the scheme.

Existing Practices for Land Assembly

The limitations of the CPO process make it difficult to create a climate of partnership and consensus. Even when the political will among the local planning
authorities makes the CPO option viable, the delays and risks of the process often
deter the private sector. Other routes to assemble land by persuasion are difficult
to apply in a strategic way and often fail to achieve satisfactory land assembly,

---

1. The progress of this Planning and Compensation Bill is recorded in Appendices C and D.

but a complementary approach that builds on the strength of each may provide an answer.

The complementary approach outlined in this chapter draws upon research reported in a discussion paper selectively released by the Urban Villages Forum of the Prince's Foundation in February 2001 (UVF 2001), concerned with the potential contribution of the process known as land pooling to the land assembly problem.[2]

Land Pooling

As things stand, if a public authority wishes to acquire land for recoupment via ownership, it will do so by private contractual agreement or by CPO. But there is another way to achieve some of the objectives of acquisition for comprehensive development, redevelopment and possibly some recoupment without the authority gaining complete ownership of the property. This approach is known generally as *land pooling*, *land readjustment* or *land consolidation*.

Land pooling is when landowners combine their interests in order to participate in land assembly, servicing and disposal in accordance with a plan. Since some help is needed from government, the process is called *assisted land pooling*. It involves the initiatives and skills of the private sector in land assembly, yet it leaves landowners with a stake in their landownership, if they so wish. Assisted land pooling is new to Britain but has been adopted extensively in other countries (Doebele 1982; Larsson 1993; Liebmann 1998).[3]

The discussion paper reviews specific ways that land pooling could complement existing compulsory-purchase and voluntary routes to land assembly, particularly in situations where compulsory-purchase powers for land assembly may be limited or unavailable and where public-sector finance for doing so is nonexistent or constrained. The research suggests that assisted land pooling could be as effective in Britain as anywhere else in encouraging development, redevelopment and rehabilitation in accordance with planning hopes and expectations. It is argued that this would be achievable by a suitable vehicle, tailored to British requirements. The research proposed such an authorised framework, which would aim to persuade owners to participate in joint action for successful land assembly for development or redevelopment.

---

2. The discussion paper is based on research commissioned by Linklaters & Alliance, DETR, and the Urban Villages Forum (later the Prince's Foundation). The research was led by research director Nathaniel Lichfield, and the rest of the team included: Owen Connellan, Denzil Millichap, Stuart Black, Ray Archer and Dalia Lichfield. Tim Dixon, director of research at the College of Estate Management in Reading, prepared the discussion paper. Its contents represent the views of the study team and do not necessarily reflect the views of the funding bodies.

3. These implementations were researched in detail, with the assistance of numerous local experts acting as country correspondents, for the discussion paper (UVF 2001).

Recommended Process for Land Pooling in Britain

The findings in the discussion paper (UVF 2001) as reviewed by Connellan (2001a; 2002b) regarding assisted land pooling are as follows.

Assisted Land Pooling

A legitimate and efficient system of assisted land pooling will:

- actively promote partnership;
- produce a fair and equitable sharing of profit and risk among willing and unwilling landowners;
- have a decision-making framework that is speedy, fair and efficient in its outputs and processes;
- address issues of acquisition and disposal values and property rights; and
- leave social and environmental issues to the political process of planning.

Lessons from Other Countries

Assisted land pooling has achieved these objectives in other parts of the world via a wide spectrum of mechanisms, categorised as:

- entirely voluntary, conceived de novo, for achieving land assembly by agreement among owners (analogous to U.K. practice in the private sector);
- public-authority inspired, controlled and compulsorily effected (German model);
- voluntary but having recourse to an authorised framework (French model);
- authorised framework designed on majority rules (overriding dissenters and enforcing participation) and instigated by a nucleus of owners (Japanese model).

Successful land pooling schemes in other countries share an element of compulsion from authorities. The French and Japanese models are of particular interest because they combine and integrate voluntary and compulsive elements. Although these versions of assisted land pooling differ, all share these characteristics:

- knowledge and advice on the land pooling process are readily available;
- schemes are acceptable to the planning/local authority;
- schemes are economically viable, either in terms of market economics or with the aid of subsidy;
- schemes are backed by a required majority of owners with any dissenting minority disempowered;
- sufficient incentives for landowners, by way of either expectations of profits or reallocation of acceptable plots, as well as safeguards for risk avoidance and ultimate tax benefits;

- public authorities' requirements for exactions of any land, such as planning gain, impact fees, and the like, are not so demanding as to negate the incentives to owners and development organisations;
- development organisations are involved in schemes from the beginning, underwriting the risks and organising economical, efficient and effective development processes;
- the process for determining compensation (i.e., share apportionment, plot reallocation, or buying out dissenters) is acceptable and rapid, within minimum scope for disputes between affected parties; and
- recommended schemes must be sufficiently all-embracing and flexible to accommodate complex political factors.

Applying Assisted Land Pooling in Britain
Certain key issues must be considered in developing a suitable vehicle and framework for land pooling in Britain:

- parties will buy into the joint action if they expect favourable terms (compensation, profits, relocation, tax benefits, etc.) or if they fear being left behind as the scheme goes forward;
- if a required majority is in favour of a plan that is acceptable to the planning authority, the residual minority cannot abort the scheme;
- dissenters should be dealt with on an equitable basis (i.e., no less favourably than under compulsory acquisition); and
- owners (on any composite redevelopment scheme) should be able to avoid risk by involving a development organization early in the process as an active participant and an acceptor of risk—which will obviously mean sharing profits with that organisation.

Recouping Development Value from Land Pooling
The obvious advantage of land pooling, for public authorities, is that the desired planning and development of a particular area can be achieved without the delays and expense of compulsory-acquisition procedures, in which the public authority is exhaustively involved. The planning authority can also secure other benefits for the public within the development scheme, such as land for infrastructure, roads, green spaces, communal use and low-income housing, as well as finance resource land (land for resale to provide operational capital for the project). Some of these methods are analogous to planning gain procedures and may be considered as forms of value capture but hardly as recoupment via ownership, as the public authority in a land pooling scheme usually serves as a facilitator rather than as a purchaser of the land required for the scheme. The

value captured would take the form of the comprehensive development that would not otherwise arise.

If an authority seeks significant financial recoupment, it has to become more involved in the process and thus be able to claim a larger shareholder stake in the process on behalf of the public, with a commensurate participation in the shareholders' profits from the venture. However, it is important that a public authority's requirements not become too onerous, because the cooperation and participation of owners depends on their expectations of realised equity to themselves.

In the German model of land pooling, public authorities increase equity share via greater involvement in the process, including positive action in land readjustment and purchase where necessary. It operates through a procedure of land readjustment known as *Umlegung*, which involves subdividing land with respect to location, shape and size according to development and micro-zoning plans and other building laws; providing land for development facilities (transport, parks and green areas) from all owners equally; and maintaining the basic substance of landownership (Doebele 1982, 180). Stages of this complicated procedure are outlined in Annexe 7 to this chapter.

Although the process is a form of compulsory land readjustment carried out by local authorities in order to realise development and micro-zoning plans, it can be initiated before development and zoning plans have even been inaugurated. Originally, these powers for readjustment only applied to plots of undeveloped land, but in more recent decades, the law has been broadened to include developed properties. Similarly, the application of *Umlegung* has expanded from its original application to residential development sites and is now proving especially applicable to industrial and commercial areas and other mixed-use developments (Doebele 1982, 180).

Summary

Recoupment via purchase is one of the complementary methods of value capture, but unlike other methods, it is not strictly a form of taxation but an act of public policy that ensures that future land value growth is captured for the benefit of the community.

The British government has proposed ways to deal with the difficulties of compulsory purchase through its green-paper consultations and in Part 7 of its latest Planning and Compulsory Purchase Bill,[4] but the suggestion of land pooling as a new way forwards for land assembly for major developments is still unresolved.

---

4. See Appendices C and D for updates on these measures (now contained in the government's latest Planning and Compensation Bill) and their progress through Parliament.

■ ANNEXE SEVEN

German Model of Land Pooling (Readjustment): Umlegung

Dieterich et al. (1993, 66–67) subdivide the complicated process of *Umlegung* into the following stages:

1. The municipality makes the formal decision to start the procedure by determining the area of the *Umlegung*.

2. The rights and claims of all plots within the area of the *Umlegung* are established and added together.

3. Land designated for streets, other public space or similar amenities in the local plan is appropriated from the area of the *Umlegung*.

4. The remaining private properties are returned to all of the owners involved using a special *Verteilungsmaßstab* (standard of distribution). Standards of redistribution can be formulated according to either plot values or sizes. The size standard is only suitable to use if the values of all former plots are fairly similar. The principle of allocation has to take into account the former ratio of ownership, so that if, for example, a landowner possessed in total 20 percent of the overall value of all former plots, he should receive back 20 percent of the value of the reallocated plots.

5. New plots are allocated to landowners on the basis that each gets one or more developed plots according to entitlement, with monetary compensation if necessary.

6. When using the value-based *Verteilungsmaßstab*, the landowner has to pay the difference between the value of his former plot (undeveloped) and the value of his serviced new plot after the procedure of the *Umlegung*, whose process incidentally permits the municipality to retain betterment value (Müller-Jökel 1997). When using the *Verteilungsmaßstab* according to the sizes of the plots, the municipality is allowed to retain land equal to the increase in value caused by the *Umlegung* itself; however, according to the *BauGB*, this may not be more than 30 percent in greenfield areas and 10 percent in inner-city locations. In these calculations, the former appropriation for streets etc. (referred to in stage 3) also has to be taken into account.

CHAPTER TWELVE

Recoupment of Betterment by Capital Levy

This chapter, contributed principally by Nathaniel Lichfield, is based on Lichfield and Connellan's working paper *Land Value and Community Betterment Taxation in Britain: Proposals for Legislation and Practice* (2000a).

Introduction

Another method of LVT outside the ambit of annual taxation is capturing capital value by recouping development gains, but herein it is assumed that there is no appetite in present Labour Party circles to repeat the failed experiments tried by various post–World War II Labour governments.

What is favoured (following Prest 1981) is the introduction of an enhanced capital gains tax (CGT), coupled with a greenfield tax, which would help redress the balance of previous disappointments in attempting to recoup betterment for the benefit of the community by capital levy.

Background Review

Three different approaches to capital levies legislated by former Labour governments—the development charge of the Town and Country Planning Act (1947), the betterment levy of the Land Commission Act (1967), and the Development Land Tax (1976)—were scrapped after a comparatively short period by succeeding Conservative governments. Thus, no machinery was left for collecting betterment for the community. A tax on development gains (as opposed to the general capital gains tax already extant) was the only scheme for land value capture ever introduced by a Conservative government (in 1973). It in fact survived in principle when the incoming Labour government of 1974 adopted the proposal under the title development gains tax (DGT) for a limited period until it was superseded by development land tax (DLT) in 1976.

Would it be appropriate to revive any of these four approaches, either singly or in combination, but modified with the benefit of experience? The answer would appear to be *no* for the three major Labour innovations and *yes* for the combined Conservative/Labour DGT. The reasons are varied.

The DGT/CGT, introduced by a Conservative government and applied by Labour, fits more acceptably into the bilateral approach of capital gains taxes enacted earlier in the U.K. by the Finance Act of 1965. The 1965 act allowed the taxation of capital gains from the disposal of assets, including land, whether by outright sale or by the grant of a lease. As such, it has continued as an enduring feature of the British taxation system, except that it is now seen as part of general taxation and is not specific to land itself. Accordingly, some alternative approach is now looked for.

Incorporating the Capital Gains Approach

Prior to the merging of capital gains on land with general taxation, the DGT was conceived by the Conservative government and enacted in the Finance Act of 1974 by the succeeding Labour government. The complex process of tax calculation is summarised as follows:

> With effect from 17 December 1973 "Development Gains Tax" was charged whenever there was a "disposal" or "notional disposal" of land or buildings with development value or development potential. The incidence of the tax, and the amount of chargeable gain, were derived from the application of a mathematical formula.
>
> The taxable gain was the least of the following.
>
> 1. The disposal proceeds less 120% of the cost.
>
> 2. The disposal proceeds less 110% of the current use value at the date of disposal.
>
> 3. The full gain less the increase in current use value over the period of ownership, or since April 1965, where land was owned before that date.
>
> In making these calculations a "threshold" of £10,000 (£1,000 in the case of companies) with relief up to £20,000 (£2,000 in the case of companies) was allowed. Gains calculated in accordance with this formula were taxed at Corporation Tax rates in the case of companies, and at Income Tax rates in the case of individuals. Any gains not subject to Development Gains Tax under the formula would be subject to Capital Gains Tax. In effect general and specific betterment were being distinguished with the charge to tax being made first on the specific and then on any general betterment remaining.
>
> DGT became chargeable where there was a disposal of the taxpayer's interest in the land and buildings concerned. In addition, a chargeable event occurred where material development had been carried out, and the buildings were subsequently let. In these circumstances the "first letting" was to be treated as a disposal for the purposes and as giving rise to Capital Gains Tax and to DGT.

DGT was superseded from 1 August 1974 by Development Land Tax (DLT). (MacLeary 1991, 136–137)

Extending Capital Gains Tax

Prest (1981, 176) favours working with the extant CGT, rather than introducing any revised version of DGT. We support the idea of such an extension of an existing mechanism for capturing land gains, which has recently been given a sharper edge by the amendment of the indexing procedures (see Chapter 3). If specific types of land deals were to be subjected to special taxation, it would be necessary to bring in amended legislation, perhaps an enhanced form of CGT as a higher level of tax for such targeted transactions, and make special provisions to avoid rollover procedures and with restrictions on offsetting losses (see Chapter 10).

Basically, CGT is a tax on disposals (generally calculated on the actual gain between acquisition and disposal prices) and obviously will not bite until the land changes hands. But some argue that an enhanced form of CGT could be targeted on an accrual basis: as capital values of land increase, such accruals could be taxed despite retention of ownership. Such a course would rely on a periodic valuation process with all the attendant administrative and appellate consequences. Other tactics could certainly be introduced, as Prest describes:

> If we are prepared to go as far as a special tax on all increments of land values, why does one need anything more that the existing capital gains tax?. . . One [objection] might be that a capital gains tax is a tax on realisations rather than on accruals and that the latter is preferable in principle. But. . . if realisation is accepted as the base for some land and all non-land gains why is anything more needed in the case of land gains associated with development? And if more is needed, one can consider various devices such as accrued interest from some critical date, a system of periodic valuation on the lines of the capital gains tax rules for discretionary trusts in the period 1965–71 or even the restoration of constructive realisation at death. If it were possible to argue persuasively that the rates of tax on land gains should be higher that for the generality of gains or that there should be restrictions on loss offsets this could be done without too much difficulty. And similarly, any demands for rollover provisions in respect of development gains or for indexation could be met by reference to existing practices or proposals in respect of capital gains generally. (1981, 177)

Greenfield Tax

Another possibility for recouping betterment is a greenfield tax on previously undeveloped land, usually outside the urban fringe. This was originally proposed by the Department of the Environment, Transport and the Regions in response to a debate that flowered suddenly, in 1998, when the rural lobby protested the possibility of dramatic encroachment on greenfield land, to build housing to accommodate some 4.4–5.5 million new households that would appear between 1995 and 2016. The proceeds of the greenfield tax would be used to subsidise development in the brownfield land, which would cost more to prepare (e.g., in dealing with contamination) and might have little or even negative value. It is also interesting that the Georgist Group on Action for Land Taxation and Economic Reform (ALTER 1998, 5) regarded a greenfield tax as an interim solution pending the full implementation of LVT.

However, while attacking a proportion of the development value released by the granting of planning permission on greenfield land would appear to be a very close cousin of the philosophy behind the three earlier Labour schemes, it can be justified by a recognition that all development rights in the country are virtually nationalised (and indeed, as such, have survived the privatisation and deregulation energies of succeeding Conservative governments). From this it could be argued that a government policy to allocate the provision of the additional homes for the predicted extra households would constitute the granting of those development rights from the national estate.

From this viewpoint, it would be quite illogical and inequitable for the government to allow the owners of the greenfield sites to reap the maximum possible development values while leaving the owners of the brownfield land to cope with the site clearance and reclamation costs, which would lead them to look for public subsidy. A more logical and equitable approach calls for the very cross-subsidisation promoted. Otherwise, the government policy to further restrict development of the greenfield sites would mean that the taxpayer would have to subsidise the brownfield land development.

A brownfield subsidy would not necessarily apply to all "previously developed land." Some brownfield land could well have a positive development value (e.g., if it were redeveloped at high density). In that case, the market could be expected to find developers. Only land with negative development value would need the subsidy. The hypothecated greenfield tax could well be a major source of gap funding to make feasible the redevelopment of brownfield land with negative development value.

Capital Gains and Greenfield Tax in Combination

A CGT on land and a greenfield tax could be imposed side by side since their purpose and incidence would be different. The capital gain on land (a form of DGT) would be levied on disposal, when the profit element had been secured, and the greenfield tax would be levied when greenfield land was developed in accordance with local planning policy. It would be justified not only because the landowner would profit from the development but also because the landowner should pay for the permission to use the state's development rights, in light of national policy. Clearly there would need to be mutual adjustments to avoid hardship, such as the charge of double taxation.

Summary

A possible addition to an annual ongoing LVT is an enhanced form of CGT perhaps coupled with a greenfield tax as a viable, contemporary method of value capture by capital levy. One reason for this proposal is that it would fit in more easily with current Labour Party thinking than past "Old Labour" ideas have.

CHAPTER THIRTEEN

Future Contributions to Infrastructure Costs

This chapter, contributed principally by Nathaniel Lichfield, is based on Lichfield and Connellan's working paper *Land Value and Community Betterment Taxation in Britain: Proposals for Legislation and Practice* (2000a; see also Appendix C for further reference).

Introduction

One way to capture value for the benefit of the community when land is being developed is to require developers to make a contribution to the community's infrastructure costs. Britain currently does this through a planning gain/obligation system, which has come under justifiable criticism. What follows is an outline of research on six possible avenues of change:

1. Elson: Code of Practice

To improve the planning gain/obligation system, Elson (1990, 42) recommended a Code of Practice that would clarify the following issues:

- the types of on-site requirement and off-site benefit seen as appropriate for different broad use categories, including mineral extraction;
- how far contributions should deal with revenue as well as capital items;
- how small-scale developments would be dealt with;
- how policies might be specified in development plans;
- the use of development briefs in negotiation;
- methods of broad financial calculation of scales of possible benefit;
- procedures for accountability and public consultation; and
- village appraisals and town surveys of local requirements.

2. Countryside Agency: Development Obligations

This approach, which defines how a development compensates for its impact on a community, would consist of three elements, as proposed by the Countryside Agency:

- policies for development obligations included within development plans (without this framework, contributions from developers would be seen as opportunistic);
- a method for calculating obligations (including suggestions of techniques for assessing environmental capital);
- a mechanism in planning law to enable and enforce the above. (1999, 7–8)

3. Urban Task Force : Environmental Impact Fees

Under the heading of "environmental impact fees," the Urban Task Force (UTF) stated:

> There is a series of wider environmental impacts which are not currently taken into account within the existing system of planning obligations and planning gains. These include:

- increased air pollution caused by increased road traffic use;
- increases in energy consumption and greenhouse gases emissions;
- the loss of countryside and landscape;
- damage to bio-diversity;
- impacts on historic and cultural resources;
- soil erosion and loss;
- pressures on waste and water management systems. (DETR 1999a, 221–223)

The UTF recommended introducing environmental impact fees to help defray the environmental costs of development.

4. The Urban White Paper

The British Government's Urban White Paper (2000, annexe) lists each of the recommendations of the UTF along with the government's response. DETR intends to issue a consultation paper on planning obligations (see Planning Green Paper referred to below).

5. Replace the Planning Gain/Obligation System with the U.S. Impact Fees System

One approach is the U.S. practice of implementing development impact fees: one-time charges against new development to raise revenue for new or expanded public facilities.

There are some advantages to the U.S. system; however, the context for implementing such a system is widely different between the two countries, and constitutional dissimilarities require differences in application. Thus, while this particular question has been discussed, the approach is not favoured for the U.K. (Grant 1982, 51–59).

6. Land Readjustment (Assisted Land Pooling)

The system known by various names, but generally described as assisted land pooling (see Chapter 12), is an alternative to acquisition by compulsory purchase (eminent domain): land is assembled for comprehensive development, but existing landowners retain some stake in the ultimate ownership of the land and its value (UVF 2001, 10).

See Appendix C for reference and comparison of subsequent ideas on infrastructure costs, including some of the issues discussed below.

Latest Government Thinking and Proposals

Planning Green Paper

The government's discussion document *Planning Green Paper* (ODPM 2001) invited comments on certain planning proposals. Regarding planning obligations, the government is reviewing one of its main proposals: local tariffs aimed at "requiring developers to bear more fully the social and environmental costs of their development."

Planning and Compulsory Purchase Bill

The Planning and Compulsory Purchase Bill was introduced in 2002 as a legislative consequence of the above green paper and consultative process, with the stated purpose of expediting the planning system. It legislates reform of the compulsory-purchase and compensation regime, including a series of necessary reforms to improve the predictability of planning decisions, speed up the handling of major infrastructure projects and provide for the introduction of business planning zones. In addition to making the planning system faster, simpler and more accessible, the government believes that these measures will help achieve sustainable development.

Summary

The government seems to be heading towards a system of locally set tariffs that look more akin to impact fees than individual negotiations for planning gain or planning obligations under planning agreements. But the detail of the government's way forward on the issue of contributions for infrastructure costs (ODPM 2002b, paras. B1–B4) has yet to be finally confirmed. However, as these measures (now contained in the government's latest Planning and Compensation Bill) progress through parliamentary stages, the position will be clarified and consequently updated in Appendixes C and D on the Lincoln Institute Web site.

CHAPTER FOURTEEN

Making LVT Compatible with Planning

T his chapter, contributed principally by Nathaniel Lichfield, is based on Lichfield and Connellan's working paper *Land Value and Community Betterment Taxation in Britain: Proposals for Legislation and Practice* (2000a; see also Appendix D for further reference).

Introduction

There is an inherent conflict between the application of land value taxation and the planning of development in any particular locality (Lichfield and Connellan 1998, 45–46). LVT, which was introduced as a concept long before government began planning land use, was necessarily based on highest and best use of the land, as defined by the prevailing land and property market. Town planning, introduced in Britain in 1909, involves the government's deliberate intervention into the market process in the interests of the community.

In order to effectively introduce LVT in Britain, the two systems will need to work together somehow.

Britain's Current Town Planning System

In general, the British planning system has much the same purpose as those practised around the world. Plans are made as a basis for implementation, and control of development is a key factor. The British system, however, currently has certain features that are singular when compared with those of other countries. First, the plans are proposed in the form of written policies, and thus are not solely dependent on maps. Second, a plan in the U.K., when approved by the appropriate authorities, does not convey development rights to the landowners. This differs from systems in the U.S. and Europe where the plan contains zoning provisions, and proposed development in accord with the plan cannot be refused permission without compensation (Davies et al. 1989).

In Britain, although land is owned by private or public individuals or bodies, the development rights are owned by the state. To exercise the development rights that are attached to land units, landowners and/or developers must obtain planning permission, supported as necessary by related planning agreements, and then carry out development subject to conditions and agreements. But in the U.K., if development permission is refused, the applicant can appeal to the secretary of state for the Department of Environment, Transport and the Regions. Since there are no established development rights, the authority is able to exercise discretion in the determination of the planning application.

The Planning and Compensation Act of 1991 signified a shift towards a plan-led system as follows:

> Where, in making any determination under the Planning Acts, regard is to be had to the development plan, the determination shall be made in accordance with the plan unless material considerations indicate otherwise. (sec. 26)

In practice, if proposed development would be in accord with the plan, then the plan-led system gives a presumption for permission and therefore, although this is perhaps still at the questionable stage, for compensation on refusal.

The Difficulty of Assessing Land Value Under the Plan

Since the British development plan does not convey development rights to the landowner, but is comprised of policies, it does not specify what type of land use is permitted. Most development plans only allocate a small number of sites for development, both on greenfield and brownfield land (i.e., previously developed) sites. In addition, development plans do not generally address existing sites, where no change is proposed. This creates confusion: a policy-based plan, which is open to interpretation, particularly when policies conflict and have different weights, does not provide a clear picture of acceptable land uses and thereby potential development value.

Regarding the changing British planning system, see Appendix D, which examines the possibilities of ameliorating such problems of interpretation.

Working Towards Compatibility

LVT can be said to be compatible with planning when land valuations are based not on the highest and best use as determined by the market, but instead on the value the land will have under the development plan. The degree of compatibility will depend on two variables:

- which planning policies are actually in effect; and
- the depth of the LVT system introduced.

One possible way to achieve compatibility is through land valuation briefs, prepared by the local planning authority and based on the policies established in the local development plan, which has already obtained approval through a statutory consultation process. The principle of such briefs is not new. Hudson (1985, 6–8) advocates the introduction of a Certificate of Development Value (CDV), which would be similar to an outline planning permission. An application could be made to the Local Planning Authority (LPA) to establish exactly what uses and in what quantum they would be allowed. The decision or valuation would not be binding on the LPA, but used until any planning permission was granted.

Influencing Implementation

LVT could be a mechanism to aid plan implementation in accord with planning policies. Tax rates in the LVT system could be varied in order to encourage or discourage development. For example, LVT might tax conservation areas at a relatively low level to increase their protection. LVT could also serve as a way to bring forward land for development. Owners of derelict sites would be taxed based on highest and best use of the land, and thus be induced to develop those areas, or pass them on to those who will.

Summary

Certain special qualities of the British planning system seem likely to hinder the establishment of LVT in Britain. In practical terms, are such anticipated problems surmountable? We have presented possible solutions for reducing the uncertainties in the planning system that are at the heart of the compatibility problem. We have also indicated other possibilities that may flow from changes the government intends to make in the planning system, which may well also work towards that end.[1]

---

1. See Appendices C and D for updates on these measures (contained in the government's latest Planning and Compensation Bill).

CHAPTER FIFTEEN

Political Prospects and Feasibility

W e now weigh the political and other group pressures that are likely to foster the entry of land value taxation into the British fiscal system. In his research into these issues, Tony Vickers drew upon the insights of a team of 10 British colleagues who visited a number of cities in Pennsylvania in March 2001 to study what lessons could be learned for Britain from the split-rate tax there. His report was published for a conference in Liverpool, England, in February 2002 (Vickers 2002a) and, in shortened form, as a Lincoln Institute working paper (Vickers 2002b). The complete version of Vickers's input—a detailed treatment of his research—appears in Appendix E; in this chapter he covers the principal issues.

Politics

Because real estate is immovable, it represents an asset to the local community, and property taxes throughout history have most often been assigned to local government. British mistrust of local government (about taxes) is possibly no greater than mistrust of national government, and few in Vickers's surveys believed that LVT would be used to replace other taxes—which LVT supporters claim is essential—rather than to supplement them.

The situation is very different in the United States, where the constitution lays down rights for all states to choose from a range of taxes. The other notable difference between the U.S. and U.K. is the proportion of local government expenditure that is levied and retained locally. In the U.K., only about 25 percent of local authorities' budgets comes from sources over which they have any control. The ratio of revenue raised locally to that raised by state and merely assigned to local government is almost exactly reversed in the U.S.: only 25 percent of local government revenue comes from nonlocal sources. This is a difference of enormous political significance, which affects the mind-set of everyone in the political process. Therefore, the potential of LVT to be an economic instrument for local government will remain much less in any part of the U.K. than it might be in other countries, until British local authorities are given greater local financial powers.

Culture

By "culture," we mean the prevailing fashion for tackling issues within public institutions, the media and civic society. Britain is no longer prone to ardent street campaigning or to radical change of any sort. But central government now uses the tool of best value to require each local authority to review all of its processes and services every five years or less. Modernisation and pilots of all sorts of policies are currently very fashionable, and debate is stifled by the prevalence of blame culture, in which every level of government seems to place responsibility on another tier for its problems and failures while claiming credit for success in its domain, whatever the cause.

Another important aspect of British culture that impedes debate about radical reform is the general belief that the experts, as opposed to politicians, are always right. This deference to authority might be challenged by environmentalism. Environmentalists are largely responsible for another cultural trend: support for hypothecation in taxes. Increasingly, people are demanding that there be an ethical case for any and all new taxation.

Economics

Economic factors are beginning to favour LVT. In Britain thus far, the officials most interested in LVT have been on the economic policy team of the Department of Environment, Transport and the Regions (now the Office of the Deputy Prime Minister [ODPM]), looking for economic instruments that support government policy objectives. The revenue-raising power of LVT is less important to them than its effect on human economic behaviour.

The Political Parties

Labour

Labour shares the liberal tradition of a strong land campaign running from when the party was originally formed until World War II. Labour went on to legislate three times between 1947 and 1976 expressly to capture the unearned increment of land values through taxation for public benefit.

But the failure of these efforts has had a negative effect on Labour perceptions of the benefits to the party of such policies as LVT and its ilk. Nevertheless, a significant number of young, ambitious and influential MPs at Westminster have spoken publicly in favour of LVT, and the Labour land campaign, although small, is stronger in numbers than it has been in many years.

However, the proposal to regularise the planning gain system is the nearest that New Labour policy comes to recognising the importance of recouping land value for the benefit of the community (Labour Party 1994). There is no sign of a desire to really reform property taxation, and even the promises of 1997 (Labour Party 1997) to end the capping of councils' tax-raising powers and return control of setting the Uniform Business Rate to councils have been abandoned.

With luck and skill exercised by the Labour land campaign, a solid bridge-head of committed LVT supporters in the parliamentary Labour Party could be built within the next few years.

Conservatives

The Conservative Party exists to preserve (or conserve) the privileges of the landed interests, or so runs the theory, but the party's current standing is dire, particularly over such issues as European integration. However, if the party becomes more like the European Christian Democrats, it is arguable that it could be influenced with ideas of LVT.

LVT prospects in Britain would certainly improve with a Conservative Party once again seriously challenging for power, but with an open mind on the land question. If LVT, however, remains a "left-right" issue, history shows that it is unlikely to reach, let alone remain on, the statute book.

Liberal Democrats

For the first time since it was formed in 1988, in its manifesto for the 2001 election, Britain's third party explicitly supported site value rating (Liberal Democrats 2001). A series of policy motions at Federal Party conferences has now secured a firm foothold for LVT, which some of the party's most influential economists openly and strongly support. From now on, it will almost certainly gain strength and move forward, although whether as a local or national tax is unclear. The Federal Party is due to review its entire taxation policy in 2005–2006, after the next general election.

The policy on choice for revenue raising clearly allows Liberal Democrats to support the proposals in this book, but, as Adrian Sanders MP, its Parliamentary local government spokesman, says, "This is not just a subject for debating societies. This is real politics. This is one of the most important issues on which our generation has to make a choice" (Vickers 2002c, 9).

Green Party

The role of Greens in the ongoing LVT campaign in Britain may be that of encouraging Liberal Democrats to act upon their policy of demanding pilots of LVT. The more that the Greens campaign on the issue, the more likely it is that

Green Liberal Democrats and Green-tinged politicians in all parties will pay attention to the subject.

In the Scottish parliamentary elections of May 2003, Greens campaigned with LVT as one of their top five policy priorities. They advanced from one to seven seats, indicating that LVT is certainly not a vote loser.

Nationalists

The Scottish Nationalist Party (SNP) in 1998 endorsed a policy of support "in principle" for LVT and further study of its potential. But, it is unlikely that nationalist support for LVT will be crucial unless and until they achieve their main aim, which is independence. At that point, national taxation systems will leap to the top of their agendas, but meanwhile they seem not to care too much, even about how their local councils are funded. Nevertheless, they do demand more local tax-raising powers.

Northern Ireland politics is unlike that of mainland Britain. The province has a long tradition of joined-up official thinking. The Assembly at Stormont could move faster towards LVT than anywhere in the U.K., and systems that might enable LVT will be in place by 2006. However, at the time of writing, Stormont politics is on hold, and U.K. ministers run Northern Ireland again.

The Devolution Effect

Members of the Welsh and Scottish legislatures say that they sense that their colleagues (elected and official) want to prove themselves more effective and more radical than Westminster and Whitehall and show the people who elected them that they can deliver better government through devolution. Taxation is at the heart of representative government. And land is what defines the scope of devolved government, quite literally. As one Scottish Labour politician put it, "Land reform is the most distinctive area of Scottish policy."

Devolution gives a place—not a people—its own government. English people living in Scotland, but not Scottish people living in England, have devolution. Similarly, it is Scottish property taxation for local finance that is open to debate in Scotland's Parliament, not taxation of Scottish-earned income or profits.

British local government is really local administration of central government, so little power does it have to fund its functions. Devolution will probably change that, but it will be a painful process. Differences are already emerging within parties, based on geography and devolved powers.

Tax reform is bound to be at the heart of any changes in politics in a devolved Britain.

Nonparty Politics

In its constitutional and land reform conventions, Scotland has exhibited almost a bicameral formality about involvement of nonparty, nonelected civic bodies in the political process. Whitehall imposes on councils and many of its other creature bodies (ministries and quasi-autonomous nongovernmental organisations [QUANGOs]) an obligation to consult with, and even form partnerships to deliver services by, voluntary and/or private sectors.

This politicises a much larger number of people than before, even if it does not greatly empower them, because the rules and important spending decisions are still made by governments. But the involvement of nongovernmental organisations (NGOs) in politics is a two-way process. NGOs are becoming very adept at getting their own issues to take priority with elected politicians. Some NGOs have larger memberships and budgets than political parties, including many with an interest in land policy, such as Friends of the Earth (FoE), the Council for the Preservation of Rural England, the National Trust and the National Farmers Union.

The political prospects for LVT will be measured in the next few years by how many such NGOs (trade unions, faith groups, charities and single-issue ginger groups) come out in its favour. The international links that such NGOs have, often all the way up to the United Nations, make a success for LVT in one country resonate quickly elsewhere. The Internet helps in a similar way.

LVT Prospects

Prospects for LVT are better than they have been in decades. However, there is still very little knowledge about it. LVT's chances might be better if it were an entirely new idea, not one with an ancient history.

The most important task for proponents of LVT is to educate those who influence politicians and their official advisers. A clear, costed, low-risk method of piloting the policy must be devised and sold to those who would most benefit from it. There are almost certainly far more potential winners than losers if the right policy path is plotted.

A great deal more work is needed before Britain is ready for more than a few pilots of LVT. But the political climate is as suitable as it ever has been. The best prospect for a real start is probably in Scotland, where there is a formal commitment by the reelected Labour/Lib Dem Executive to investigate LVT as the replacement for council tax. However, pilots could begin in any part of the U.K. where a strong-enough local campaign can be put together, with national support from a wide coalition of NGOs and professional bodies.

Summary

Various current pressures are accumulating for a change in taxation in Britain, particularly towards a more equitable distribution of the rates burden (property tax) and thus a fairer collection of local government revenue. They arise from the present incidence of devolving governing and taxation powers to Scotland, Wales and Northern Ireland and from the activities of various influential special interest and political groups (e.g., Greens, Scottish Nationalists, Liberal Democrats and even active Georgist organizations). Such influences now enhance the argument that it is both timely and appropriate to contemplate an introduction of LVT, particularly into Britain.

CHAPTER SIXTEEN

Final Review: What Does All This Mean and How Important Is It?

W here have we arrived in our examination of LVT as affecting these relatively small islands off the coast of mainland Europe? Our response and our goal in this final chapter is to bring together substantial issues from the British experience of land value taxation and its future prospects into fuller context.

Part I: Introduction

In this section, we examined the nature of LVT in its two basic forms (site value rating [SVR] and capital levies for value capture) and noted the essential difference between them: an annual tax (such as SVR) should pick up all increases in land value over time; the one-off hits by value capture exactions only consequent upon certain trigger events (e.g., an act of development process or property demise).

The prospects for the introduction of LVT in Britain are encouraging, as is its prospective importance in the current movement towards taxation shift. LVT is thus potentially part of the change that favours those taxes, such as eco-taxes, that tackle the problem of charging for the use we make of land (in its widest aspects) and its consequential environmental effects, instead of taxing enterprise wages, profits and production.

The intellectual underpinning of LVT can be traced to the economic and moral thinking of the early French Physiocrats and an array of classical economists. But, it is the American social philosopher and economist Henry George who made the greatest impact in his seminal work *Progress and Poverty* (1879). He argued persuasively for a single tax on land and the abolition of other taxes, which then were predominantly levied on other property. George felt land values were based exclusively on general forces, whether of a natural or social character. Landlords had no moral right to land values, and there was no case for their retaining existing rents or the increments that were likely to accrue in the future as economies expanded. The case for LVT that emerges is as follows: first, the tax is based on the land's economic rent, which is morally justified in that its value has not been created by the landowner; second, the tax is efficient because it is economically neutral, as it does not affect the supply of other goods and services; and third, landowners cannot shift the tax.

Part II: The British Experience

After analysing the history and present circumstances of the rating (property tax) system, taken together with our overview of the general taxation system in Britain, we considered how LVT (or SVR) might harmonise within the extant British taxation systems, taking into account the influence of membership of the European Union. It appears that there is no real impediment to introducing LVT, either as a replacement tax or even as an additional tax.

It has been helpful to examine how LVT[1] has been tried in varying aspects over the history of Britain. Since the nineteenth century, there have been many attempts to introduce some form of site value taxation, and various government committees have pronounced on its possibilities. There has also been post–World War II interest in reviving those attempts right up until the present day, and we have reviewed and analysed their successes and failures. Despite more than a century of social, economic and political pressures, successive governments have had a distinct lack of success in bringing LVT within their armoury of tax-gathering measures to supplement local and national revenues. This is due, in part, to opposition from various professional groups and landowners, each with their own taxation agendas. Modern economists have not supported George's root-and-branch single-tax panacea, although proposals under consideration by Parliament certainly did not embrace these in their original form. Rating valuers and surveyors have stressed the difficulties of site valuation (despite the findings of the Whitstable pilot surveys) and still hold to the long-established rating procedures for a tax on the occupation of combined hereditaments of both land and buildings.

In evaluating LVT as a capital exaction influencing development activities, we first considered recoupment of development value via ownership, sometimes known as land banking, which we include under the overall descriptive term as LVT. As a means of land value capture for the benefit of the community, this process gained impetus in the years immediately following World War II, and hence we treat it as an historical precursor to later attempts at value capture. Governments can recoup development value by early ownership of land. We have concentrated our analysis on the British history of land acquisition, but use exam-

---

1. Here we are addressing the tax in its simplest form, being the process of raising an annual tax on land values, usually to meet some elements of government expenditures. Other forms of LVT, such as recoupment via ownership, development value capture and recovery of infrastructure costs are referred to later.

ples from other countries to illustrate the process, which is exercised in various forms all around the world.

One of the most important ways to capture value for the community is the recoupment of betterment via the town and country planning system. Here, betterment refers to increased value from development activity, in line with the Uthwatt Committee's view that "[t]he principle of betterment [legislation] is that the public authority are entitled to require the owner of land increased in value by their works to pay over in money part of the increase which he hereby enjoys" (1942, 116).

However, three postwar measures for betterment tax as a capital levy on development value in Britain, introduced by successive Labour administrations, were all withdrawn by succeeding Conservative administrations, and to date no really comparable legislation has replaced them. Why did these measures fail? We agree with Blundell (1993, 12–13) that they were very complex pieces of legislation, and unintended anomalies arose. Furthermore, they were preoccupied with speculative profits made at a given point in time and not with taxing a continuing accumulation of land values. Overall, the combined effect was to provoke resistance or inertia, to deter development and the better use of land, to encourage land hoarding by owners and to produce an artificiality of sites.

One critically important feature of the original Town and Country Planning Act (1947) remains unaffected: the Crown continues to own all landed property development rights, and these rights have not been returned to the property owners. Consequently, there is now no compensation problem; if a planning application is refused, or is granted with conditions, there can be no claim for loss of development rights. This lends considerable support to the case for revisiting LVT in Britain.

Among the ways of capturing development value for the community, we are particularly concerned with the recovery of contributions to infrastructure costs. We have found the current situation unsatisfactory, based on exactions determined by planning gains and planning obligations. This should be the occasion for new thinking, including some recent suggested measures that have yet to be fully considered by Parliament.

As previously indicated, the second part of this book reviews the complex history of land taxation in Britain. Since the end of Roman occupation up to the nineteenth century, land taxation as such has never been of major importance as an actual or potential fiscal or taxation tool of government. More relevant to our considerations are the various attempts since the 1880s to promote the introduction of LVT. But of the many attempts to introduce an annual land tax, only two acts of Parliament reached the Statute Book, in 1910 and in 1931, and both were allowed to lapse before making any positive impact. However, to recap, these attempts were directed towards annual ongoing taxes, i.e., termed site value rating in Britain, and not to capturing value for the benefit of the community on the occasion of development. Apart from unsuccessful attempts to secure betterment as part of the planning process in 1909, 1925 and 1932, various development taxes were introduced from 1947 onwards—development charge, betterment levy, development gains tax and development land tax. But all these measures were repealed by successive governments.

Although these capital levies were abandoned, there still remain other extant ways of recouping some development value back to the community. Recoupment via purchase can be exercised as a form of land banking by public authorities for planning purposes, and exactions known as planning gains or planning obligations are obtainable from developers to offset some public infrastructure costs. However, a capital gains tax, enacted in the U.K. by the Finance Act of 1965, allowed the taxation of capital gains made on the disposal of assets, including land from outright sale or the grant of a lease. As such, it has been an enduring feature of the taxation system, now seen as part of general taxation and not specifically related to land.

We recognise that the many past efforts by British governments to introduce a measure of land taxation equity, through SVR for local government revenues, and for recouping capital values to the community on the occasion of development, met with only very limited success, and most proved difficult to administer in practical terms.

Part III: Opportunities for Future LVT

Our hope is that by learning from past endeavours, we can present proposals that avoid previous shortcomings and so pave the way to a more acceptable future for LVT in its broadest applications. We began by looking at options available for introducing LVT into Britain at the present time and choices from which we can make recommendations. What emerged from this analysis is the case for gradualism; the success of new and changed land taxation depends on steady progression rather than challenging confrontation.

We accordingly propose that Britain should make an initial venture into LVT by way of site value rating, replacing the current property tax (rating) system with a two-rate basis following the Pennsylvania model. This would entail splitting existing assessments between an owner's rate on the land and an occupier's rate on improvements, with a gradual transition to a full owner's rate on site value only at highest and best use (on a development plan-led basis). At the same time, unrated and unoccupied land would be brought into the SVR system. The question of capital levies (value capture) is a separate issue, but clearly related to LVT.

The practical implications of an annual LVT to replace the current business rates was discussed with regard to Vickers's research (see Appendix B) that analysed the technical and administrative measures necessary for the introduction of LVT. Implementation proposals for smart-tax pilot schemes in selected parts of the U.K., perhaps coupled with BIDs, could act as tests for national adoption of LVT in the future.

Recoupment via public ownership is another means of capturing land value growth for the benefit of the community. We also have considered the British government proposals to deal with the difficulties of compulsory purchase (eminent domain), but recognise the need for new approaches to land assembly, land pooling and public-private equity sharing for major developments.

There is clearly no appetite in present Labour Party circles to repeat those failed experiments with betterment levies by various Labour governments since World War II. However, introduction of an enhanced capital gains tax coupled with a greenfield tax would fit more easily with current Labour Party thinking and offer more political feasibility. The full detail of such proposals of planning gains/obligations is not entirely clear (despite the presentation of the latest Planning and Compulsory Purchase Bill), but it seems to herald at least a prospect of the U.S. style of impact fees. However, for further enlightenment we can only wait upon events (see updates in Appendices C and D).

We have considered whether the British planning system will prove a hindrance to the establishment of LVT in Britain or whether such potential problems are resolvable. The anticipated changes in the planning system confirmed in the recent Planning and Compulsory Purchase Bill may well also work towards that end. One of the major underlying issues in establishing LVT in Britain concerns the political pressures likely to affect its introduction, no matter how strong the pragmatic and moral cases may be. We addressed those political and other influences that may shape prospects for LVT in Britain, as highlighted in Vickers's research (see Appendix E).

Why Is LVT Particularly Relevant Now?

Various current pressures are accumulating for a change in taxation, particularly towards a more equitable distribution of the rates burden (property tax) and thus a fairer collection of local government revenue. These arise from the incidence of devolving governing and taxation powers to Scotland, Wales and (when eventually restored) Northern Ireland and also from the activities of various special political groups (e.g. Greens, Scottish Nationalists, Liberal Democrats and even active Georgist organisations). Besides the possibility of reintroducing capital levies, there is also a sense that the current methods of capital value capture, i.e., recoupment via purchase and contributions for infrastructure, need to be strengthened and augmented; recent government pronouncements have added to expectations in these areas.

Pulling the Threads Together: Where We Are

The crux of our concluding argument is that the political prospects are opportune and feasible for the introduction of site value rating as a form of LVT, initially on a dual-rate basis that will also extend the tax base to empty, unused and derelict land. This could eventually replace, on a transitional basis, the current property tax (rating) system for local revenues. There are also opportunities for extending LVT to include increased capital exactions on development activity, namely an enhanced capital gains tax, possibly bolstered by a greenfield tax. Other opportunities involve augmenting the land banking process and contributions for infrastructure costs.

But what would be the expected benefits of taxing land value in these various ways?

- *Economic:* LVT cannot be shifted and will not distort economic activity. Nor will it discourage building and improvement. It will produce revenue with less economic burden than other taxes.
- *Efficiency:* LVT would be cheaper, quicker and easier to assess, to bill and to collect from landowners.
- *Effectiveness:* LVT is more effective as a taxation instrument than current rates (property tax) and council tax in Britain for exacting contributions towards government expenditures, because it is a tax on owners rather than on occupiers and because it is a tax on land only. As an annual tax, it is an effective means of capturing increases in land value, which occur because of community actions.
- *Equity:* Taxing landowners on their land values is an equitable means of extracting "value capture" from wealth and even incomes that have not been earned by those landowners. This value is arguably created by the community in various ways over time and is something that should and could be recouped for the benefit of the community by way of LVT. Empty, unused and derelict land should bear a charge that reflects its value as a social asset.

What does all this mean? And how important is it? We need to look further than these listed opportunities and consider LVT as part of a larger tax shift.

Eco-taxes

Eco-taxes[2] are increasingly viewed as part of such a taxation shift. Their compatibility with LVT, in terms of their social and economic relationships, has previously been examined by Lichfield and Connellan (2000c). Their working paper considered the distinct nature of the two forms of taxation and the link between them, and the possible application of LVT to supplement eco-taxation. The conclusion is that these two forms of taxes, although different in history and application, should be able to live together in mutual harmony and interdependence. Details of this argument can be found in an abridged version of the working paper in Appendix F and Connellan (2000b).

Some particular issues from that paper are elaborated as follows:

Link Between LVT and Eco-taxes

A general overriding reason for links between the taxes has been introduced by Robertson: "policy makers should seriously examine the potential of the site-value tax, as a resource tax which will contribute to economically efficient, socially equitable, and environmentally sustainable developments" (1999, sec. 3.1). Robertson's reasons, which reflect the views of many others, argue for a tax shift from "enterprise and employment and onto resources including land, energy and the capacity of the environment to absorb pollution" (sec. 3.2).

The Affinities and Their Relevance to Sustainability Issues

We assume that LVT would have general application. What then would be its effect on the environment? If the assessments reflect the planning system, then green spaces within urban areas will be assessed at their present use and exclude value for future development. If the assessments follow market expectations, then the retention of such green spaces can be encouraged by scaled reductions in the tax or even exemptions. In other words, the imposition of LVT need not necessarily encourage development, although in specific cases that may be desirable. This same principle of tax amelioration might be applied to areas outside the urban fringes when preservation of the countryside is a policy aim.

At the same time, the general imposition of LVT would encourage development within urbanised areas and mitigate the tendencies towards sprawl at the urban edges with a beneficial effect on the green spaces beyond. The classic

---

2. Eco-taxation here follows the definition used by the European Commission (ATW Research 1996), namely, that it is based on a physical unit (or proxy for it) of something that has proven specific negative impact on the environment. It can be a tax (unrequited payments to government) or a charge (requited payments for which a service is provided by some public body generally in proportion to payment made), and these are examples of economic and financial instruments, which are designed to modify market behaviour with a view to achieving government objectives (DETR 1993).

Georgist argument can be updated to address the current green issues: urban development can lessen the pressures to expand beyond the urban fringe. In addition, revenues garnered from such LVT could be used for the amelioration of pollution and redemption of other eco-transgressions. This, in turn, raises the issue of sustainability and sustainable development,[3] and leads us to consider the degree to which LVT and eco-taxation are consistent with those concepts. It is not difficult to argue the case, since eco-taxation can be regarded as a natural offspring of the International Union for Conservation of Nature and Natural Resources (IUCN 1980) and World Commission on Environment and Development (1987). Its primary purpose is to ensure that the quality of the environment is conserved for future generations, even though this implies diminution of the product from contemporary development.

Perhaps it is less easy to show that LVT in itself is sustainable in this sense. For one thing, while the concept of conservation was around when LVT was introduced to the world through Henry George, the concept of sustainability was not. Indeed, doubts have arisen as to whether LVT as envisaged by George can be seen as "green," because it could stimulate development on open space that should be protected into the future, and also stimulate the premature release of farmland for development and encourage the related speculation in doing so. This apparent conflict stems from the inherent incompatibility between the system of LVT, which follows the market in making the assessments related to the highest and best use that can be obtained, and public policy, which aims to regulate the market in the public interest, as for example in the conservation of open land, natural amenities and beauty, and coastal zones.

In order to ensure compatibility between LVT and regulation, we introduce the concept of the regulated market (see Appendix D). This means that the assessments of land value for LVT are based not on the unregulated market known to Henry George in the nineteenth century, but on the regulated market of those countries that have subsequently introduced planning regulation and economic instruments in order to protect the environment. If this situation is to be the basis for the LVT assessment, then LVT must be green, insofar as the plans and policy instruments of the locality in question are also green.

In summary, the introduction of LVT can be seen as compatible with the armoury of green taxes, and as a widening of the concept of how we could order our institutions to serve our sustainable interests for future generations.

Pressures for Restructuring the Tax System

General arguments for systemic tax reform are gaining support. They include:

---

3. Sustainable development is defined as "meeting the needs of the present without compromising the ability of future generations to meet their own needs" (WCED 1987).

- reducing distortionary taxes on business enterprise and human effort would benefit the economy;
- greater efficiency in the use of natural resources (now overused) and in the use of human resources (now underemployed and underdeveloped) could be achieved;
- unemployment would be reduced by lowering taxes for both employees and employers;
- reduced energy use, other natural resource use and pollution would benefit the environment; and
- developing capacities and skills would exploit the growing world market for environmental technologies.

Towards a Tax Shift

A taxation shift away from enterprise, production and income sources and towards the cost of using the environment is connected to sustainability and the sustainable development argument. Some policies include eco-tax reform and site value land taxation, based on:

- the introduction of a range of taxes and charges on the use of common resources and values, including, but not limited to, energy and the site value of land; and
- the reduction, and perhaps the eventual abolition, of taxes and charges on employment, incomes, profits, value added and capital; together with
- less heavy tax on the incomes and profits they earn from useful work and enterprise, on the value they add, and on what they contribute to the common good; but
- heavier taxes and charges reflecting the value they subtract by their use of common resources, including land, energy and the capacity of the environment to absorb pollution and waste (Robertson 1999, sec. 3.0).

Two important American reports are among recent publications that have discussed in depth the need and scope for a tax shift on those lines. Hamond et al. do not specifically include LVT among their recommendations, but they underline LVT's compatibility with them.

> Reconciling healthy economic development with the protection of the air, water and natural habitats is one of the great challenges of the next century. A revenue-neutral shift to resource taxes offers a way to help to meet this challenge. A resource tax could work somewhat like a rental or interest payment for the use of assets that are owned by all of us, ranging from the broadcast spectrum to the air we breathe. These new revenues would, by reducing other taxes that are a drag on the economy, provide a dividend—lower taxes on work and saving—to which the public is entitled.

These environmental levies would not impose a sudden charge for things that used to be available at no cost, as some people will protest; rather they would extend the effort to end "free lunches" to perhaps the biggest free lunch of all: free or low-cost use of assets owned by everyone in common. (Hamond et al. 1997, ch. 4)

In the other American report, Durning and Bauman give a prominent role to LVT as a sprawl tax, which they treat as one of five major types of desirable tax (the others being carbon, pollution, traffic and resource consumption taxes). The following indicates the approach they support:

> Most Northwest jurisdictions seek to prevent sprawl through the regulatory tools of land use planning; none applies taxes to the same task. Yet a simple reform to the existing property tax would turn it into a powerful incentive for investment in city and town centers and in adjacent neighborhoods.
>
> A property tax is actually two conflicting taxes rolled into one. It is a tax on the value of buildings and a tax on the value of the land under those buildings. As experience in Australia, New Zealand, Taiwan and Pennsylvania shows, shifting the tax from the former to the latter aids compact development while suppressing land speculation, promoting productive investment, and tempering housing costs, especially for the poor. (Durning and Bauman 1998, 2–3)

Conclusion

The taxing of land in particular can have far-reaching repercussions beyond its immediate fiscal importance. In our consideration of the case study of Britain we have seen the many different attempts to introduce various measures of land value taxation as influenced primarily by the teaching of Henry George. From this analysis, we looked to future prospects for the tax in Britain and even to wider shores.

We conclude that it is now appropriate to contemplate an introduction of LVT, especially into Britain. Various current pressures can be identified as accumulating for a change in taxation, particularly towards a more equitable distribution of the rates burden (property tax) and thus a fairer collection of local government revenues. These also include widening the tax base to bring in properties presently unrated and not caught up in the present British property tax, e.g., empty, derelict and unused properties. In addition, we envisage present opportunities for introducing capital levies such as an enhanced capital gains tax. Such pressures arise from the devolving governing and taxation powers to Scotland, Wales and (when eventually resinstated) Northern Ireland and also to the activities of various influential special interest and political groups (e.g. Greens, Scottish Nationalists, Liberal Democrats and even active Georgist organisations).

All of this is set against a current background of taxation shift away from production and on to various exactions that could be made for the use and abuse of natural resources, including land. Here we are entering the realms of eco-taxation and issues affecting the sustainability of the planet, but we have suggested that LVT ought to be considered as having a rightful place among these important measures currently under debate. So, it is entirely appropriate now to repeat a quotation from Solow:

> The best way to keep George's ideas alive and effective is to develop and refine them, and to extend their range of relevance to issues of land use, urban form, and taxation, including many aspects that could never have crossed George's mind. The range of possible activities is very broad. . . . The list could be very long; this random selection is intended to indicate only how diverse it could be. (1997, 14)

His statement reminds us that we are dealing with still-developing ideas that require continuous re-examination for their relevance to modern and changing circumstances. The significance of the emerging issues almost speaks for itself, and LVT is seen, by its supporters at least, as an ideal vehicle to encourage new approaches to taxation at perhaps an historical turning point.

We remember, however, that Henry George in the nineteenth century was realistic, even cautious, about progress:

> The truth that I have tried to make clear will not find easy acceptance. If that could be, it would have been accepted long ago. If that could be, it would never have been obscured. . . . Will it at length prevail? Ultimately yes. But in our own times, or in times of which any memory of us remains, who shall say? (1879, 214)

Responding from the twenty-first century, shall we not ponder that perhaps at last that time has come?

Glossary
INCLUDING ACRONYMS & LEGISLATION

ad hoc	to this; formed, arranged or done for a particular purpose
ad valorem	according to value
Barnett formula	formula for distributing government grants to U.K. regions
best value	the term coined by New Labour government to describe obligatory market testing and internal audit of local government services by councils, with various incentives for good performance
betterment	amount of increase in the value of land due to development prospects
brownfield	potential redevelopment site within the urban fringe, often formerly industrial and contaminated
capitalisation	process whereby the present value of an income (as affected by taxation) is converted into the capital value of an asset
chain shops	multiple stores owned by retail groups frequently found in shopping outlets
compulsory purchase	process whereby public authorities are given statutory powers to acquire landed property under an authorised basis of compensation (in the U.S., see *eminent domain*)
conveyancing	transfer of legal title for real estate
corporeal	having a physical or substantial presence, e.g., real estate

council tax	hybrid property/poll tax levied on all residential properties in Britain
de novo	anew; starting from the beginning
economic rent	amount of payment above what is necessary to keep a factor or person in their present employment
eco-taxes	taxes based on a physical unit (or proxy for it) of something that has a proven, specific negative impact on the environment
eminent domain	the right of a government or its agent to expropriate private property for public use, with payment of compensation (see *compulsory purchase*)
European Council	grouping of the heads of government of the European Union
European Union	economic and political association of 15 European countries, currently in process of expansion (to 25 members), as a unit with internal free trade and common external tariffs
ex gratia	as an act of grace, not compelled by legal right
Fabian Society	A left-wing political group, founded in Britain in 1884, working towards the gradual rather than revolutionary achievement of socialism
green belt	planning process of inhibiting the spread of urban development into the countryside
greenfield	potential development site outside the urban fringe
greenfield tax	taxation proposal to levy taxes on development permitted beyond existing urban fringes
Green Paper	U.K. government consultation document
hereditament	item of property that can be inherited; used in U.K. rating parlance to identify units of property taxation
hypothecation	for a specified purpose, e.g., allocation of taxation receipts

inclosures	historical U.K. legal process of enclosing land for private use as opposed to public access
Inland Revenue	the part of Treasury responsible for implementing U.K. tax laws
inter alia	among other things
land banking	acquisition process of assembling ownership of land in advance of development requirements
Land Recycling Fund	proposal by the authors to use revenue from LVT/ VLT as loans to developers for site remediation
Lib Dem(s)	shortened form for Liberal Democrat Party, the third largest British political party, or its members
listed building	building protected from any development that alters its historic features, as defined in detailed official lists
Local (Unitary) Plan	statutory planning document prepared by every local authority in Britain, setting out policies to be followed as the basis for development control by the Planning Authority
millage	one-thousandth part (of a dollar)
New Deal	the term (originally U.S. usage) coined by New Labour to include a range of policies to tackle social and economic exclusion of individuals and communities
Physiocrats	group of French economic thinkers who propounded land value tax theory in the eighteenth century
plan-led	recommended valuation practice to ensure that assessed values for LVT purposes accord with authorised development plan policies and proposals
planning gain	planning practice to recoup some form of capital gain to the community from developers as part of the development process
planning obligation	formal agreement entered into by a planning authority and a developer to ensure strict performance of obligations as a fundamental part of the planning permission granted

poll tax	name given to community charge, a per capita tax on individuals used from 1988 to 1993 in Britain for part of local government revenue, but now replaced by council tax
prima facie	on first view
quinquennial	every 5 years
rates	form of British property tax, currently levied on annual values of nondomestic properties
rebus sic stantibus	as things stand
rollovers	taxation process of carrying forward gains and/or losses from the disposal of one asset to the acquisition of another
Royal Prerogative	Right of the Crown that, in British Common Law, is theoretically subject to no restriction in intervening and circumventing normal constitutional and administrative processes, and is usually delegated to the government or the judiciary
Shadow Cabinet	Opposition party team of Members of Parliament that "shadow" government ministers
sine qua non	an essential condition; something absolutely necessary
smart tax	term used by supporters of the split-rate tax in some Pennsylvania cities and adopted for a similar proposal in U.K.
subsidiarity	the principle that a central authority should have a subsidiary function, performing only those tasks that cannot be performed at a more local level
Supplementary (Business) Rate	Business rate proposal by government in 2000 Green Paper to allow councils to levy small extra rate on business occupiers
sustainability	conserving an ecological balance by avoiding depletion of natural resources

sustainable	"meeting the needs of the present without compromising the development ability of future generations to meet their own needs" (WCED 1987)
terra firma	firm earth, i.e., the ground as distinct from the sea and air
Tory(ies)	sobriquet for the U.K. Official Opposition, the Conservative Party, or its member(s)
Treasury	The U.K. government's finance department
Treaty of Rome	International Agreement (1957) setting up the framework of the European Economic Community (later becoming the European Union)
Unitary Plan	see *Local Plan.* Unitary local authorities are those with no county tier; the district assumes county functions
Whitehall	overall mode of reference to centralised British civil service

ACRONYMS

BID	Business Improvement District
BRC	British Retail Consortium
CAMA	computer-assisted mass assessment
CAP	Common Agricultural Policy of the European Union
CBI	Confederation of British Industry
DETR	Department of the Environment, Transport and the Regions; large Whitehall department of State, responsible for local government, regional economic development, planning, housing and urban renewal policy until 2001 (replaced by the DTLR)
DNF	Digital National Framework

DTLR	Department of Transport, Local Government and the Regions; slimmed-down successor to DETR, created in June 2001 and retaining responsibility for urban renewal and most planning functions
FoE	Friends of the Earth; environmental campaigning NGO
GIS	geographic information system
GLA	Greater London Authority; regional government for London introduced in 1999
HGF	Henry George Foundation
HMLR	Her Majesty's Land Registry
HMSO	Her Majesty's Stationery Office
IdeA	Improvement and Development Agency; wholly owned consultancy arm of local government in England and Wales
IULVT	International Union for Land Value Taxation
JCC	Joint Cabinet Committee between Labour and Liberal Democrat Parties, formed in 1997 to help guide constitutional reform
LIT	Local income tax
LVT	Land value tax (taxation)
MEP(s)	Member(s) of the European Parliament, which meets in Strasbourg, France
NGDF	National Geo-spatial Data Framework
NGO	nongovernmental organisation
NLIS	National Land Information Service
NLPG	National Land and Property Gazetteer
OcR	Occupiers Rate

ODPM	Office of the Deputy Prime Minister
OLT	Owners Land Tax
OS	Ordnance Survey, the British national mapping organisation
PAYE	Pay As You Earn; automated system for collecting income tax and national insurance payments at source, used by all employers in U.K. and Inland Revenue
PC	Plaid Cymru, the Welsh nationalist party
QUANGO	Quasi-autonomous non-governmental organisation; a semi-public administrative body outside the civil service but with financial support from and senior appointments made by the government
SDLT	Stamp duty land tax; replaces stamp duty as of 1 December 2003
SNP	Scottish National Party
SRVC	Scottish Rating and Valuation Council
SVR	site value rating
TCPA	Town and Country Planning Association
UBR	Uniform Business Rate
UTF	Urban Task Force; set up in 1998 by the deputy prime minister to report on policies for urban renewal
VOA	Valuation Office Agency; department of the Inland Revenue, tax arm of Treasury that values real estate for tax purposes
VLT	Vacant Land Tax

LEGISLATION

TCPA1932	Town and Country Planning Act, 1932
GPPA1944	Gas Petroleum (Production) Act, 1944
TCPA1944	Town and Country Planning Act, 1944
NTA1946	New Towns Act, 1946
TCPA1947	Town and Country Planning Act, 1947
CIA1949	Coal Industry Act, 1949
TDA1952	Town Development Act, 1952
OCA1958	Opencast Coal Act, 1958
LCA1961	Land Conception Act, 1961
CSA1964	Continental Shelf Act, 1964 (for off-shore)
TCPA1968	Town and Country Planning Act, 1968
TCPA1971	Town and Country Planning Act, 1971
LGPLA1980	Local Government, Planning and Land Act, 1980
OGEA1982	Oil Gas (Enterprise) Act, 1982 (for on-shore)
PCA1991	Planning and Compensation Act, 1991
LGFA1992	Local Government Finance Act, 1992
TCPA1997	Town and Country Planning Act, 1997

References

Acolia, G.R. 1984. The enigmatic entrepreneurial profit factor. *Property Tax Journal* (March):21–25.

Action for Land Taxation and Economic Reform (ALTER). 1998. *Submission to finance sub-group of the local government policy review of the Liberal Democrat party.* London: ALTER.

Adam, S., and C. Frayne. 2001. Briefing note 9: *A survey of the UK tax system.* London: Institute of Fiscal Studies. www.ifs.org.uk/taxsystem/taxsurvey2001.pdf. (This paper substantially revises and updates the U.K. chapter by A. Dilnot and G. Stears in K. Messere, ed., *The tax system in industrialised countries.* Oxford: Oxford University Press.)

Adams D., A. Disberry, N. Hutchison, and T. Munjoma. 1999. Do landowners constrain urban development? Report papers in *Land Economy*, 99–101 (March):36 pp. Aberdeen: Aberdeen University.

Alterman, R., ed. 1988. *Private supply of public services: Evaluation of real estate exactions, linkage and alternative land policies.* New York: New York University Press.

American Institute of Real Estate Appraisers (AIREA). 1987. *The appraisal of real estate,* 9th ed. Chicago: AIREA.

Andelson, R.V., ed. 1997. *Land-value taxation around the world,* 2nd ed. New York: Schalkenbach Foundation.

———. 2000. *Land-value taxation around the world,* 3rd ed. Malden, MA: Blackwell Publishers.

Ashworth, W. 1954. *Genesis of modern British town planning.* London: Routledge and Kegan Paul.

ATW Research. 1996. Manual: Statistics on environmental taxes. In *Environmental taxes and green tax reform.* Paris: Organisation for Economic Co-operation and Development.

Bailey, C.D., R.E. Lake, W.G.E. Ormond, and H.T. Wright. 1967. *The general rate.* London: Rating and Valuation Association.

Barker, L.A. 1955. *Henry George.* Oxford: Oxford University Press.

BBC Business News. 2000. *Europe's mobile phone rollercoaster.* 23 October. London: BBC. http://news.bbc.co.uk/1/hi/business/986428.stm.

Blundell, V.H. 1993. *Essays in land economics*. London: Economic and Social Science Research Association.

Brandon, P. 2002. Livingstone rival links local democracy and land value. *Land and Liberty* 109(1203):4.

Britton, W., O. Connellan, and M.K. Crofts. 1991. *The cost approach to valuation: A research report for the RICS*. Kingston: Kingston Polytechnic.

Brown, H. James, ed. 1997. *Land use and taxation: Applying the insights of Henry George*. Cambridge, MA: Lincoln Institute of Land Policy.

Bryden, J., 2001. Plenary speech at *Getting to the root: Scotland, Russia and land value taxation,* conference at Pollock Halls, Edinburgh, 9 July.

Callies, D.L, and M. Grant. 1991. Planning for growth and planning gain: An Anglo-American comparison of development conditions, impact fees and development agreements. *The Urban Lawyer* 23(2):221–248.

Clarke, P.H. 1965. Site value rating and the recovery of betterment. In *Land values,* report of the proceedings of a colloquium of the Acton Society Trust, London, 13–14 March, Peter Hall, ed., 73–96. London: Sweet and Maxwell Limited.

Claydon, J., and B. Smith. 1997. Negotiating planning gains through the British development control system. *Urban Studies* 34(12):2003–2022.

Connellan, Owen. 1997. *Land (site) taxation: An international perspective*. Toronto, Canada: IAAO International Conference.

———. 1998. *Re-introducing land value taxation in Britain?* Orlando, FL: IAAO International Conference.

———. 1999. *Land value taxation (LVT) within the European Union*. Las Vegas: IAAO International Conference.

———. 2000a. Land value taxation: New opportunities for Britain and Europe? *Journal of Property Tax Assessment and Administration* 5(2):17–32.

———. 2000b. *Can land value taxation (LVT) aid and supplement eco-taxes?* Edmonton, Canada: IAAO International Conference.

———. 2001a. *Land assembly for development: Something borrowed, something new?* From RICS research conference, *The cutting edge*. Oxford: Royal Institution of Chartered Surveyors (RICS).

———. 2001b. *Will Britain follow Pennsylvania with a split-rate property tax?* Miami: IAAO International Conference.

———. 2002a. *Land assembly for development: The role of land pooling, land readjustment and land consolidation*. Washington, DC: FIG 2002 International Conference.

———. 2002b. *Land value taxation in the 21st century: Opportunities for Britain*. Los Angeles: IAAO International Conference.

Connellan, Owen, William J. McCluskey, and Anthony Vickers. 1998. *The surveyor's role in land value taxation.* Brighton, U.K.: FIG 1998 International Conference.

Connellan, Owen, Frances Plimmer, and William J. McCluskey. 2003. *LVT: An international prospect?* Helsinki: European Real Estate Society (ERES) International Conference.

Council Tax (Alteration of Lists and Appeals) Regulations 1993 (SI 1993 no. 290), as amended.

Council Tax (Contents of Valuation Lists) Regulations 1992 (SI 1992 no. 553).

Council Tax (Exempt Dwellings) Order 1992 (SI 1992 no. 558), as amended.

Council Tax (Situation and Valuation of Dwellings) Regulations 1992 (SI 1992 no. 550).

Countryside Agency. 1999. *Planning for quality of life in rural England.* Cheltenham: Countryside Agency.

Cox, A. 1984. *Adversary politics and the land: The conflict over land and property policy in post-war Britain.* Cambridge: Cambridge University Press.

Cullingworth, J.B., and V. Nadin. 1994. *Town and country planning in Britain.* London: Routledge.

Davies, H.W.E, D. Edwards, A.J. Hooper, and J.V. Punter. 1989. *Planning control in Western Europe.* London: Her Majesty's Stationery Office (HMSO).

Denman, D., and S. Prodano. 1972. *Land use: An introduction to proprietary land use analysis.* London: Allen and Unwin.

Department of the Environment (DoE). 1983. *Circular 22/83: Planning gain.* London: HMSO.

Department for Environment, Food and Rural Affairs (DEFRA). 2000. *Greater protection and better management of common land in England and Wales.* London: HMSO. http://www.defra.gov.uk/wildlife-countryside/consult/common/01.htm.

Department of the Environment, Transport and the Regions (DETR). 1988a. *SI (Statutory Instrument) 1999/1199: The town and country planning (assessment of environmental effects) regulations.* London: HMSO.

———. 1988b. *Modernising local government: Business rates.* London: HMSO

———. 1989a. *Draft guidance: Planning agreements.* London: HMSO.

———. 1989b. *The town and country planning (assessment of environmental effects) regulations.* S1 1199. London: HMSO.

———. 1989c. *Environmental assessment: Guide to the procedures.* London: HMSO.

———. 1991. *Circular 16/91: Planning obligations.* London: HMSO.

———. 1993. *Making markets work for the environment.* London: DoE.

———. 1994 *Planning and pollution control.* London: HMSO

———. 1995. *Circular 11/95: The use of conditions in planning permissions.* London: HMSO.

———. 1997a. *Circular 1/97: Planning obligations.* London: HMSO.

———. 1997b. *Planning policy guidance: General policy and principles.* London: HMSO.

———. 1997c. *The operation of compulsory purchase orders.* Report by the City University Business School. London: HMSO.

———. 1997d. *Planning policy guidance no. 1: Principles.* London: HMSO.

———. 1998. *Planning for the community for the future.* London: HMSO.

———. 1999a. *Fundamental review of the laws and procedures relating to compulsory purchase and compensation: Interim report.* London: DETR.

———. 1999b. *Towards an urban renaissance: The report of the urban task force chaired by Lord Rogers of Riverside.* London: Routledge. www.detr.gov.uk.

———. 2000a. *Our towns and cities: The future: Delivering an urban renaissance, cm 4911.* London: DETR.

———. 2000b. *Fundamental review of the laws and procedures relating to compulsory purchase and compensation: Final report.* London: DETR.

———. 2000c. *Modernising local government finance: A green paper.* Department of Transport, Local Government and the Regions. http://www.local.detr.gov.uk/greenpap/part2.htm.

Department of Transport, Local Government and the Regions (DLTR). 2001. *Making local government finance fairer: Timetable.* News release 336, 20 July. http://www.voa.gov.uk/news/press01/council_tax_reval.htm.

Dieterich, H., E. Dransfield, and V. Winrich. 1993. *Urban land and property markets in Germany.* London: UCL Press Ltd.

Doebele, William A., ed. 1982. *Land readjustment: A different approach to financing urbanization.* Lexington, MA: D.C. Heath and Co.

Douglas, Roy. 1976. *Land, people and politics: A history of the land question in the United Kingdom, 1978–1982.* London: Allison and Busby.

Durning, A., and Y. Bauman. 1998. *Tax shift: How to keep the economy, improve the environment and get the tax man off our backs.* Seattle: Northwest Environment Watch.

Elson, M. 1990. *Negotiating the future: Planning gain in the 1990s.* Chipping Sodbury: ARC Aggregates Ltd.

Emeny, R., and H.M. Wilks. 1984. *Principles and practice of rating valuation,* 4th ed. London: Estates Gazette Ltd.

Encyclopaedia Britannica, 15th ed. 29 vols. 1997. Chicago: Encyclopaedia Britannica Inc.

Essex, Sue. 2003. Sue Essex announces new council tax valuation bands. Press release. National Assembly for Wales. 24 September.

Evans, B., and R. Bate. 2000. *A taxing question: The contribution of economic instruments to planning objectives.* London: Town and Country Planning Association.

Expert Committee on Compensation and Betterment. *See* Uthwatt Committee 1942.

Feldstein, M.S. 1977. The surprising incidence of a tax on pure rent: A new answer to an old question. *Journal of Political Economy* (April):249–360.

Fibbens, M. 1995. Australian rating and taxing: Mass appraisal practice. *Journal of Property Tax Assessment and Administration* 1(3):61–77.

Field Place Caravan Park Ltd. v Harding (VO) [1966] 3 All ER 247.

Gaffney, M. 1994. *Land as a distinctive factor of production.* In *Land and taxation,* N. Tideman, ed. London: Shepherd-Welwyn.

George, Henry. 1879. *Progress and poverty.* Centenary edition, 1979. New York: Robert Schalkenbach Foundation.

German, C.G., D. Robinson, and J. Youngman. 2000. Traditional methods and new approaches to land valuation. *Land Lines* (newsletter of Lincoln Institute of Land Policy) (July): 4–5.

Gibbon, Edward. 1951. *Decline and fall of the Roman Empire.* 6 vols. London: J.M. Dent and Sons Ltd.

Gloudemans, R.J. 2000. Implementing a land value tax in urban residential communities. *Journal of Property Tax Assessment and Administration* 5(4):17.

Graham, M. 1986. *Land taxation.* London: Sweet and Maxwell.

Grant, M. 1982. False diagnosis, wrong prescriptions. *Town and Country Planning* 51(3): 59–61.

———. 1999. Compensation and betterment. In *British planning: 50 years of urban and regional policy,* Barry Cullingworth, ed. London: Athlone Press.

Grayson, R. 1999. *Funding federalism.* London: Centre for Reform.

Greater London Authority (GLA). 2001. Q1. Green-land values. In *Transcript of mayor's question time 18 July 2001.* London: GLA.

Hagman, Donald, and Dean Misczynski, eds. 1978. *Windfalls for wipeouts: Land value capture and compensation.* Chicago: American Society of Planning Officials.

Hamond, M.J., S.J. Decarrio, P. Duxbury, A.H Sanstad, and C.H. Stinson. 1997. *Tax waste, not work: How changing what we tax can lead to a stronger economy and a cleaner environment, redefining the programme.* http://www.redefiningprogress.org/publications/pdf/TaxWaste_sum.pdf.

Hansard. 1909. *Official report of proceedings of British Parliament,* 29 April. London: HMSO.

Harrison, Fred. 1983. *The power in the land: Unemployment, the profits crisis and the land speculator*. London: Shepheard-Walwyn.

———. 2002. The first major political breakthrough in 50 years for the rent-as-public-revenue policy at national government level is now on the cards. *Georgist News 5* (12 September). www.progress.org.

Hartzok, A. 1997. Pennsylvania's success with local property tax reform: The split rate tax. *American Journal of Economics and Sociology* 56(2):207–214.

Healey, P., M. Purdue, and F. Ennis. 1992. *Gains from planning: Dealing with the impacts of development*. Oxford: Oxford University Press.

Heap, Desmond. 1996. *An outline of planning law*, 11th ed. London: Sweet and Maxwell.

Henderson, Hazel. 1994. Paths to sustainable development: The role of social indicators. *Futures* 26(2):125–137.

———. 1999. *Beyond globalization: Shaping a sustainable global economy*. Bloomfield, CT: Kumarian Press.

Her Majesty's Stationery Office. 1976. *Local government finance: Report of the committee of inquiry* (Cmnd 6453). London: HMSO.

———. 1981. *Alternatives to domestic rates* (Cmnd 8449). London: HMSO.

———. 1983. *Rates—Proposals for rate limitation and reform of the rating system*. London: HMSO.

———. 1986. *Paying for local government* (Cmnd 9714). London: HMSO.

———. 1991. *A new tax for local government*. London: HMSO.

Hicks, J.R. 1959. Unimproved value rating—The case of East Africa. In *Essays on world economics*. Oxford: Oxford University Press.

Hudson, P.R. 1995. *Administrative implications of site value rating*. London: Land and Liberty Press.

Huhne, C. 1990. *Real world economics*. London: Penguin Books.

International Valuation Standards Committee (IVSC). 1986. *International valuation standards*. London: IVSC.

———. 2000. *International valuation standards*. London: IVSC.

———. 2001. *International valuation standards*. London: IVSC.

———. 2003. *International valuation standards*. London: IVSC.

International Association of Assessing Officers (IAAO). 1990. *Property appraisal and assessment administration*. Chicago: IAAO.

International Union for Conservation of Nature and Natural Resources (IUCN). 1980. *The world conservation strategy*. Gland, Switzerland: IUCN.

Jacobs, M. 2000. *Paying for progress: A new politics of tax for public spending.* Report of the Commission on Taxation and Citizenship. London: Fabian Society.

Jennings, Ivor W. 1946. *The law relating to town and country planning,* 2nd ed. London: Charles Knight and Co. Ltd.

John Laing and Son Ltd. v Kingswood Assessment Committee (1949) 1 All ER 224.

Johnson, T., K. Davies, and E. Shapiro. 2000. *Modern methods of valuation,* 9th ed. London: Estates Gazette Ltd.

Jones, T. 1972. *The case for site value rating.* London: Liberal Party.

Kay, J.A., and M.A. King. 1990. *The British tax system,* 5th ed. Oxford: Clarendon Press.

Kehoe, Dalton, ed. 1976. *Public landownership: Framework for evaluation.* Lexington, MA: D.C. Heath and Co.

Khan, S.A., and Frederick E. Case. 1976. *Real estate appraisal and investment.* New York: Ronald Press Co.

Labour Party. 1994. *In trust for tomorrow.* London: Labour Party.

———. 1997. *New labour: Because Britain deserves better.* London: Labour Party.

Land Value Tax Campaign. 1996. *Practical politics.* Brentwood, U.K.: LVT Campaign 64 (July).

Larsson, G. 1993. *Land readjustment.* Aldershot, U.K.: Avebury (Ashgate Publishing Group).

Law Commission. 2001. *Compulsory purchase and compensation: A scoping paper.* London: Law Commission.

Lawrence, E.P., B. Newton, and K.C. Kearns. 1992. *George and democracy in the British Isles.* New York: Robert Schalkenbach Foundation.

Layfield Committee. 1976. *Report of a committee of inquiry into local government finance.* London: HMSO.

Lee, G. 1996. *The people's budget: An Edwardian tragedy.* London: Henry George Foundation.

Liberal Democrat Campaign for Land Value Taxation. 1997. *Land in a liberal democracy.* Oxford: Hebden Royal Publications.

Liberal Democrats. 1998. *Moving ahead: Towards a citizens' Britain.* London: Liberal Democrat Party.

———. 1999a. *Re-inventing local government: Competent, powerful and free.* London: Liberal Democrat Party.

———. 1999b. Policy motion F13: Choice for revenue raising. In *Autumn 1999 conference agenda.* London: Liberal Democrat Party.

———. 2000. *Engaging communities: Proposals for urban regeneration in England.* London: Liberal Democrat Party.

———. 2001. *A real chance for real change.* London: Liberal Democrat Party.

Lichfield, D. 1990. Planning gain: In search of a concept. *Town and Country Planning* 56(6):178–180.

Lichfield, N. 1956. *The economics of planned development.* London: Estates Gazette Ltd.

———. 1989. From planning gain to community benefit. *Journal of Planning and Environment Law* (January):68–81.

———. 1991. Alternative approaches to funding infrastructure. In *Seminar: Planning gain and section 106 agreements: The new regime.* London: University College London and Legal Studies and Services Ltd.

———. 1992. From planning obligations to community benefit. *Journal of Planning and Environmental Law* (December):1103–1118.

———. 1992a. The integration of development planning and environmental assessment. Part 1, Some principles. *Project Appraisal* 7(2):58–66.

———. 1996. *Community impact evaluation.* London: UCL Press.

Lichfield, N., and D. Lichfield. 1992. The integration of development planning and environmental assessment. Part 2, A case study. *Project Appraisal* 7(3):175–185.

Lichfield, N., and O. Connellan. 1998. Land value taxation in Britain for the benefit of the community: History, achievements and prospects. Working paper. Cambridge, MA: Lincoln Institute of Land Policy. www.lincolninst.edu/pubs/workingpapers.asp.

———. 2000a. Land value and community betterment taxation in Britain: Proposals for legislation and practice. Working paper. Cambridge, MA: Lincoln Institute of Land Policy. www.lincolninst.edu/pubs/workingpapers.asp.

———. 2000b. Land value taxation for the benefit of the community: A review of the current situation in the European Union. Working paper. Cambridge, MA: Lincoln Institute of Land Policy. www.lincolninst.edu/pubs/workingpapers.asp.

———. 2000c. Land value taxation and eco-taxation: Their social and economic inter-relationship. Working paper. Cambridge, MA: Lincoln Institute of Land Policy. www.lincolninst.edu/pubs/workingpapers.asp.

Lichfield, Nathaniel, and Haim Darin-Drabkin. 1980. *Land policy in planning.* London: George Allen and Unwin Ltd.

Liebmann, George W. 1998. *Land readjustment for America: A proposal for a statute.* Cambridge, MA: Lincoln Institute of Land Policy.

Lipsey, R.G. 1989. *An introduction to positive economics,* 7th ed. London: George Weidenfeld and Nicolson Ltd.

London Docklands Development Corporation (LDDC). 1998. *Regeneration statement.* London: LDDC. www.lddc-history.org.uk.

Longman. 1984. *Dictionary of the English language.* Harlow: Longman Group UK, Ltd.

Loughlin, Martin. 1985. Apportioning the infrastructure costs of urban land development. In *Land policy: Problems and alternatives,* Susan Barret and Patsy Healey, eds. Aldershot, U.K.: Gower.

Lovelock, J. 2000. *Gaia: A new look at life on Earth.* Oxford: Oxford University Press.

Macdonald, C. 2001. Speech by Calum Macdonald MP, at *Getting to the root: Scotland, Russia and land value taxation,* conference at Pollock Halls, Edinburgh, 9 July.

MacLeary, A.R. 1991. *National taxation for property management and valuation.* London: E&FN Spon.

McAuslan, J.P.W.B. 1984. Compensation and betterment. In *Cities, law and social policy: Learning from the British,* Charles M. Haar, ed., 77–87. Lexington, MA: D.C. Heath and Co.

McCluskey, William J., and A.S. Adair. 1997. *Computer assisted mass appraisal: An international review.* Avebury: Avebury Publishing Limited.

McCluskey, William J., and Riel C.D. Franzsen. 2001. Land value taxation: A case study approach. Working paper. Cambridge, MA: Lincoln Institute of Land Policy. www.lincolninst.edu/pubs/workingpapers.asp.

McCluskey, William J., Frances Plimmer, and Owen P. Connellan. 2002. Property tax banding: A solution for developing countries. *Assessment Journal* 9(2):37–47.

Mill, J.S. 1998. *Principles of political economy,* Jonathan Ridley, ed. Oxford: Oxford University Press.

Millichap, Denzil. 1999. Land assembly for comprehensive planning and development for major development projects: Historic background of the CPO system. Report of research group; unpublished.

Müller-Jökel, R. 1997. *The development of the legal land adjustment system in Germany— Consequences for developing countries.* Paper presented at the 9th International Seminar on Land Readjustment and Urban Development, Bangkok, Thailand.

Nelson, A.C. 1988. *Development impact fees.* Chicago: Planning Press.

Netzer, Dick, ed. 1998. *Land value taxation: Can it and will it work today?* Cambridge, MA: Lincoln Institute of Land Policy.

Noke, C. 1979. The reality of property depreciation. *Accountancy* 90(1035):129–130.

Non Domestic Rating (Alteration of Lists and Appeals) Regulations (SI 1993 no. 291).

Non Domestic Rating (Unoccupied Property) Regulations, 1989 (SI 1989 no. 2261), as amended.

Oates, W.E., and R.M. Schwab. 1997. The impact of urban land taxation: The Pittsburgh experience. *National Tax Journal* L(1).

Office of the Deputy Prime Minister (ODPM). 2001. *Planning green paper: Planning delivering a fundamental change.* London: ODPM.

———. 2002a. *Compulsory purchase powers, procedures and compensation: The way forward.* London: ODPM.

———. 2002b. *Reforming planning obligations: Delivering a fundamental change: Initial regularity impact assessment.* London: ODPM.

———. 2002c. *Sustainable communities—Delivering through planning.* London: ODPM.

O'Riordan, T., ed. 1997. *Eco-taxation.* London: Earthscan.

Parker, H. Ronald. 1965. The history of compensation and betterment since 1900. In *Land values,* Peter Hall, ed., 53–72. London: Sweet and Maxwell Ltd.

Planning Advisory Group. 1965. *The future of development plans.* London: HMSO.

Planning and Law Reform Working Group of Society for Advanced Legal Studies. 1998. *Report.* London: Society for Advanced Legal Studies.

Plant Commission. 2000. *Paying for progress: A new politics of tax for public spending.* London: Fabian Society.

Plato. 1955. *The Republic,* H.D.P. Lee, trans. Harmondsworth, U.K.: Penguin Books.

Plimmer, Frances. 1998. *Rating law and valuation: A practical guide.* London: Addison Wesley Longman.

———. 2000. The council tax: The need for a revaluation. *Journal of Property Tax Assessment and Administration* 5(1):27–40.

Plimmer, Frances, William J. McCluskey, and Owen P. Connellan. 2000a. *The British domestic property tax: A banded solution for other countries?* IAAO International Conference, Edmonton, Canada, September.

———. 2000b. Equity and fairness within ad valorem real property taxes. Working paper. Cambridge, MA: Lincoln Institute of Land Policy. www.lincolninst.edu/pubs/workpapers.asp.

Prest, A.R. 1981. *The taxation of urban land.* Manchester: Manchester University Press.

Price, J.W. 1994. *Mellows: Taxation of land transactions.* London: Butterworths.

R v Paddington (VO) ex parte Peachey Property Corporation Ltd. (1965) RA 177.

Raphael, D.D. 1985. *Adam Smith.* Oxford: Oxford University Press.

Ratcliffe, John. 1976. *Land policy: An exploration of the nature of land in society.* London: Hutchinson and Co.

Rees, W.H., ed. 1988. *Principles into Practice*, 3rd ed. London: Estates Gazette.

Ricardo, David. 1951. *The works and correspondence of David Ricardo*. Vol. 1, *Principles of political economy and taxation*, Piero Sraffa, ed. Cambridge: Cambridge University Press.

Roberts, Neal Alison. 1977. *The government as land developers: Studies of public land-ownership policy in seven countries*. Lexington, MA: D.C. Heath and Co.

Robertson, J. 1998a. Resource taxes and green dividends: A combined package? In conference proceedings, *Sharing our common heritage, resource taxes & green dividends*. Oxford: Oxford Centre for the Environment, Ethics and Society.

———. 1998b. Sustainable development: The role of rent. *Land and Liberty* 105(1185): 7–11.

———. 1999. *The new economics of sustainable development: A briefing for policymakers*. London: Kogan Page.

Robinson, Dennis. 1991. Interactions between land policy and land-based tax policy. In *International conference proceedings 1991*. Cambridge, MA: Lincoln Institute of Land Policy.

Roots, G. 1993. *Ryde on rating*. London: Butterworth.

Rosslyn Research. 1990. *Planning gain: A survey for KPMG*. London: Peat Marwick.

Royal Commission on the Distribution of the Industrial Population (RCDIP) (Barlow Report). 1940. *Report*. London: HMSO.

Royal Institution of Chartered Surveyors (RICS). 1964. *The rating of site values: Interim report of a working party*. London: RICS.

———. 1985. *The private finance initiative: The essential guide*. London: RICS.

———. 1991. *Statements of asset valuation practice and guidance notes*. London: RICS

———. 1995. *Appraisal and valuation manual*. London: RICS.

———. 1996. *The Bayliss report: Improving the rating system*. London: RICS.

———. 1997. Letter agreeing to a record of a meeting between liberal democrat MP David Rendel and Charles Partridge FRICS, chair of local rating panel of RICS, March.

Saxer, Shelley Ross. 2000. Planning gain, exactions and impact fees: A comparative study of planning law in England, Wales and the United States. *The Urban Lawyer* 32(1):21–71.

Scarrett, D. 1991. *Property valuation: The five methods*. London: E&FN Spon.

Schnidman, Frank. 1988. Land adjustment: An alternative to development exactions. In *Private supply of public services: Evaluation of real estate exactions, linkage, and alternative land policies*, Rachelle Alterman, ed. New York: New York University Press.

Schumpeter, Joseph A. 1954. *History of economic analysis*. Oxford: Oxford University Press.

Scottish Office. 1999. *Land reform policy group: Recommendations for action*. Edinburgh: Stationery Office.

Secretary of State for the Environment. 1990. *Our common inheritance*. London: HMSO.

Shenkel, W. 1978. *Modern real estate appraisal*. New York: McGraw-Hill.

Simes Committee of Enquiry. 1952. *The rating of site values*. London: HMSO.

Smith, A. 1776. *The wealth of nations*. Chicago: University of Chicago Press.

Smith, S. 1995. *Green taxes and charges: Policy and practice in Britain and Germany*. London: Institute for Fiscal Studies.

Society for Advanced Legal Studies. 1998. *Report of working group on planning obligations*. London: Society for Advanced Legal Studies.

Solow, Robert M. 1997. How to treat intellectual ancestors. In *Land use and taxation: Applying the insights of Henry George*, H. James Brown, ed. Cambridge, MA: Lincoln Institute of Land Policy.

Southgate, M. 1998. Sustainable planning in practice. *Town and Country Planning* 67(11): 332–342.

Stanlake, G.F. 1989. *Introductory economics*, 5th ed. Harlow: Longman Group UK, Ltd.

Stigler, G.J. 1969. Alfred Marshall's lectures on progress and poverty. *Journal of Law and Economics* (April).

Strong, Ann L. 1979. *Land banking: European reality, American prospect*. Baltimore: Johns Hopkins University Press.

Turner, D.M. 1977. *An approach to land values*. Herts: Geographical Publications Limited.

Turvey, R. 1957. *The economics of real property*. London: George Allen and Unwin Ltd.

Urban Villages Forum (UVF). 2001. *Land pooling for major development projects: A discussion paper*. London: UVF.

Uthwatt Committee. 1942. *Expert committee on compensation and betterment: Final report*. London: HMSO.

Valuation and Community Charge Tribunals (Transfer of Jurisdiction) Regulations, 1989 (SI 1989 no. 440).

Valuation and Land Agency (VLA). 2004. *Frequently asked questions (revaluation 2003)*. www.vla.nics.gov.uk/rfaq.htm.

Valuation for Rating (Plant and Machinery) Regulations, 1994 (SI 1994 no. 2680), as amended.

Vickers, Anthony J.M. 1999a. *Shifting the burden*. London: Henry George Foundation.

———. 1999b. *Paying for urban renewal*. Paper for Henry George Foundation in response to Urban Task Force final report. London: Henry George Foundation.

———. 2000a. A smart way to shift taxes. *Challenge* (magazine of Green Liberal Democrats) (summer).

———. 2000b. Review of *The new economics of sustainable development* by James Robertson. *Challenge* (magazine of Green Liberal Democrats) (summer).

———. 2002a. *Lessons from the smart tax*. London: Progressive Forum.

———. 2002b. Preparing to pilot land value taxation in Britain. Working paper. Cambridge, MA: Lincoln Institute of Land Policy. www.lincolninst.edu/pubs/workingpapers.asp

———. 2002c. Shrouded in cobwebs, interview with Adrian Sanders MP. *Land and Liberty* 109(1202):6–9.

Wakeford, Richard. 1990. *American development control: Parallels and paradoxes from an English perspective*. London: HMSO.

Ward, B., and R. Dubois. 1972. *Only one earth*. Harmondsworth: Penguin.

Ward, R., J. Guilford, B. Jones, D. Pratt, and J. German. 2002. Piecing together locations: Three studies by the Lucas County research and development staff. *Assessment Journal* 9(5):15–48.

Westminster City Council v Southern Rail Co. (1936), AC 511.

Westwick, C.A. 1980. *Property valuation and accounts*. London: Institute of Chartered Accountants in England and Wales.

Whitehead, G. 1992. *Economics made simple*. London: Heinemann.

Wilks, H.M. 1964. *The rating of site values: Report of a pilot survey at Whitstable*. London: Rating and Valuation Association.

———. 1974. *The rating of site values: Update of report of pilot survey at Whitstable*. London: Land Institute.

———. 1975. *Some reflections on the second valuation of Whitstable*. London: Land and Liberty Press.

World Commission on Environment and Development (WCED). 1987. *Our common future*. New York: United Nations.

Authors' Biographies

Owen Connellan is a chartered surveyor and valuer who specialises in rating and property taxation, and is a member of the International Association of Assessing Officers (U.S.). He has worked extensively with leading professional firms in advising clients on valuation, assessment and planning matters, with commercial property organisations in implementing and managing major development projects in town centers in the U.K. and Europe. He is currently a visiting professor of Kingston University, in England, where he was formerly senior research fellow and head of school of surveying. Connellan has written and lectured widely on real property matters. His present research interests include valuation methodology and the application of information technology to asset appraisal and property taxation. He is a faculty associate at the Lincoln Institute of Land Policy.

Nathaniel Lichfield is professor emeritus of economics of environmental planning at the University of London. He is also chair at the Bartlett School of Planning, University College, London, and has taught at the University of California, Berkeley, and the Hebrew University, Jerusalem. In addition to teaching, Lichfield has practiced concurrently as planner and urban economist. He founded in 1962 Nathaniel Lichfield and Partners, Planning Development and Economic Consultants, and in 1992 joined Dalia and Nathaniel Lichfield Associates (Lichfield Planning). He has researched and published extensively over the entire range of planning and development economics.

Frances Plimmer is a senior researcher at both Kingston University, Surrey, and the College of Estate Management, Reading, England, and was formerly Reader in Applied Valuation at the University of Glamorgan, Wales. Dr. Plimmer is a chartered surveyor whose work experience began with the Valuation Office in Cardiff, dealing with rating valuation cases. She has researched extensively on rating principles and practice, in particular the fairness of U.K. real property taxes, and has supervised post-graduate research on real property taxation system in other countries. She has published and lectured extensively, particularly on the importance of understanding professional and national culture in predicting and analysing responses to externally imposed regulations. In 2002 and 2003 she was awarded a David C. Lincoln Fellowship at the Lincoln Institute of Land Policy.

Tony Vickers is a chartered surveyor who has worked on several projects to improve the way geographic information collected at public expense is made available for public benefit. He is a founding member of the Association for Geographic Information (AGI) and assists them with public affairs. Vickers began his career coordinating underground utilities on large housing sites. In 1975 he was commissioned into the Royal Engineers and spent 14 years in Military Survey. In 1995 he set up the consulting firm Modern Maps. He later was appointed chief executive of the charitable land and tax policy think tank Henry George Foundation. He has written for numerous journals on the subject of sustainable taxation and contributed to *Sustainable Civil Engineering* (John Wiley, 2001) and *Critical Issues in Environmental Taxation*, Vol. 1 (Richmond Law, 2003). He is a past recipient of a David C. Lincoln Fellowship at of the Lincoln Institute of Land Policy.

Index